# The Snake

# in the

# Dishwasher

## And 69 Other Weird

## Things That Happened

# The Snake

# in the

# Dishwasher

## And 69 Other Weird
## Things That Happened

by

Mark K. Campbell

Another book

by

Mark K. Campbell

is

SENSE VS SOUL

a novel

# THE SNAKE IN THE DISHWASHER

First printing: May 2020

Second printing: May 2020

Third printing: June 2020

Fourth printing: August 2020

Fifth printing: September 2020

IBSN: 9798633755664

*Cover image by Katie Buckel*

*Author photo by Alicia Duran*

For everyone who took the time to read
"On Your Mark …"
during its quarter century-plus run

# Contents

Preface

1. The Snake in the Dishwasher/It's Come to This   4

2. Spooky History Can't Stop Bold Creek Walkers   8

3. Hey, Buddy: Can You Spare a $1 Trillion Coin?   15

4. The History of Food Trucks in Three Playlets   18

5. Critters Hate Us and Want to Kill Us   21

6. Me and My Mammogram: What? Me Worry?   24

7. Ten Years After: I'd Love to Change the World   27

8. Sacred Sandwiches and Other Edible Miracles   30

9. Secrets to Getting the Most Out of Your Vehicle   33

10. A New Mom's Day   36

11. Attack of the Man-Breasts!   39

12. Test Tube Meat, Yum!   42

13. We Don't Need No Stinkin' Gay Bombs   44

14. When 'Bless Your Heart' Is Fightin' Words   47

15. The Sea of Love   49

16. That Snapping Is the 'Poetry of the Body'   52

17. Be the Smartest Person at Thanksgiving Again   56

18. I Love Animals, They're Delicious (!!)   58

19. If Jesus Read a Sports Column …   60

20. Here's Why We Didn't Go Home ...    64

21. What to Stash in Case Survivalists Are Right    67

22. Are You Uncouth? Take the Etiquette Quiz    70

23. Having a Gay Old Time Answering Questions    74

24. Greatest Aggie Joke: Texas A&M Israel?!    77

25. One Life ...    80

26. If it Walks/Talks Like a Duck, It Must Be Gay    83

27. Here's One of Two Terribly Wonderful Stories    87

28. The Second of Two Terribly Wonderful Stories    90

29. The Old Man and the Sea: Sea 1, Old Man 0    92

30. Verily I Say Unto Thee: Hurry Up Already!    96

31. Rock Run On    99

32. Showering with the Enemy    102

33. Analyzing a Consumer and His Consumables    105

34. A Happy Ending for Tina the Sheep    108

35. A 'Dome Lesson    111

36. A Family and Its Stump: It's at My Place Now    113

37. The Christmas Letter, Back By ~~Popular~~ Request    115

38. Stink to Think: Loving Your Body Emissions    119

39. The (Funky) Story Behind the (Stinky) Column    122

40. Generational Mind-Numbing Circumstances    125

41. Hand Jive History    128

42. Sticking a Fork into the Latest Dieting Craze    130

43. Hitting the (Sea) Wall With a 2-Year-Old Boy — 133

44. A Thanksgiving Piffle, Hold the Blasphemy — 136

45. Avoid Getting Browbeaten This Christmas — 140

46. How Many Cow Brains Could *You* Eat? — 143

47. Lessons Learned from 'The Shotgun Incident' — 147

48. What to Do if You're Inside a Giant Crab — 150

49. A Haunting Tale — 153

50. Part I: Our Early (Funky) Presidential History — 155

51. Part II: Presidential History: Florida … Again — 157

52. Part III: Presidential History: One Part to Go! — 160

53. Part IV: Hail to the End of the Pres. Series — 162

54. What Goes on While Taking Your Ambien — 166

55. Go? Go? 'Staycation' All You Ever Wanted? — 169

56. Odds on the First Woman on the $10 Bill — 172

57. Can a Song Save Your Life? — 175

58. Confession of a Transracial White Dude — 177

59. Don't Be Eyeballin' a Hippopotamus — 179

60. Duck, You Sucka! — 182

61. One Little Girl — 184

62. Lunacy? Plots for Sale on the Sea of Tranquility — 187

63. The Difference Between a House and a Home — 190

64. The True Story of the Greatest Catch Ever — 193

65. What if Social Media Existed for Historic Events — 196

66. Laying of the Hands Vs Slaying of the Toes  198

67. If You Love the Earth, Eat More Hamburgers  200

68. Color My World  203

69. A Word that Won't Die (Hint: It Starts with 'N')  206

70. A Bible Story You Likely Haven't Heard Before  210

# Preface

The original title for this book was *Surely, Ten Percent*. I figured that, maybe, ten percent of the 27-years' worth of columns I wrote were good enough for reproducing.

But, as I started wading through the 1,417 columns—one a week from Aug. 14, 1992 to Sept. 13, 2019—it became evident that 142 columns (ten percent) was going to make for a very long book since these first 70 chosen were well over 50,000 words.

The plan was for the compilation to not be some giant thing, but a tome that would lay around and be read chunks at a time. Or at the beach where no one wants to lug around some Stephen King doorstop to the seashore.

So, I began cutting it down. Some columns I knew would make the cut, pieces that readers had commented on. Others were personal favorites that I wanted to include.

All the others required rereading and that was a *lot* of rereading. It's weird to come upon something you wrote decades ago—sometimes good, sometimes what-was-I-thinking? painful.

Over 27 years, my column writing got bolder as three things occurred.

One: I spent many years writing a traditional sports column, one that I thought only sports people might like. That meant creating pieces about how the Cowboys/Rangers/Mavericks or the two local high school teams I covered were doing, stuff that didn't really stick out.

Occasionally I put in a personal tidbit or story, but for the most part, the columns were just generic—so much so, that from 1992 to 2001, only six columns made the cut for this book. (And none from 1994, 1995, and 1999.)

Then came July 6, 2001. My wife—always referred to as "the Bride" in writings—and I went on a creek hike. ("Spooky History Can't Stop Bold Creek Walkers") It was summertime, a stretch when stories for the sports pages of a pair of weekly small-town newspapers were hard to come by. The Bride and I hiked along, and I began noticing how creepy things got—animal skeletons, eerie rock formations, submerged eggs. Afterward, I wrote the piece in a snarky way, making it a jokey, pseudo-scary travelogue piece.

I almost didn't publish it because it was very left field. But, I did. And it got more positive feedback than anything I'd ever done up until then. So, that emboldened me, certainly.

Two: I became an Arlington, Texas firefighter in 1981; starting in the summer of 1992, I worked as a journalist at the same time. Those two full-time jobs were a chore, so, when the opportunity arose, I retired from the AFD after 22 years there. That gave me many more hours to ponder topics to write about, and I took advantage of it—things got sillier and more out-there from 2003 on.

Three: At the end of 2011, the publisher retired and my column, "On Your Mark ...," moved to the editorial page; finally, I was free from having to have some sort of sports tie-in (even though it was usually tenuous at best oftentimes). In May 2012, I became the two papers' editor. That meant there was literally no one to edit me—I could write whatever I wanted on anything I could think of and publish it. And, boy, did I do that!

The majority of the columns here are (supposed to be) funny. Because the publisher often wrote his weekly pieces about serious current events, I tried hard to be the opposite, to be humorous. Sometimes, however, certain unfunny topics had to be addressed—like 9/11 and family deaths.

2

However, those columns are rare. Instead, inside you'll read about man-boobs, gay ducks, bears (the world's evilest animal), barfing records, male mammograms, breastraunts, lots of irreverent religious comments (I hope you know "Come As You Are" by Nirvana)—and a battle with a snake that got into our dishwasher which leads things off.

Some columns have a "tag" at the end. That began in January 2012 when I became the editor; that's why some pieces have them and some don't.

Also, don't be put off by the spelling of "ya'll"; yes, Spell Check disagrees as much as the internet Nazi grammar/spelling police do, but I'm Texan and that's the way we *real* Texans spell it. So, don't look for a "correct," English-minor whining of "y'all"—you won't find it.

While the "ya'll" column didn't make the cut here, what follows are 70 columns—*Surely, Five Percent*—that chronicle an average guy's stretch of life from age 36 to 63.

A lot happened, as you'll see.


Mark K. Campbell
May 2020

*By far, this is the most popular column I ever wrote. Years later, if I bumped into someone on the street or a café, this was the piece they would always mention to me. It was a very weird experience and all completely true. It won a few awards. And, this was only the first of two snakes that somehow made their way into our dishwasher. This was written Sept. 9, 2004.*

# The Snake in the Dishwasher

or

# So, It's Come to This

Two disclaimers:

1) This story is a little gross.

2) PETA needn't contact me (again). I *know*.

So, here we go …

"A snake fell down on me." That's the curious sentence that began this life-awakening episode.

The Bride and I were exploring a creek bed at LBJ State Park in midsummer when my cellphone rang and our daughter said that a snake had hit her from above. She had opened the front door to let the dog out, and a snake fell down on her, bouncing off her arm.

Being a Campbell, she immediately fled, running to her room where she grabbed her dog and phone and crawled out the window. She called a couple of guys who came by to look for the reptile, but it was never found.

A month or so went by. One night at 12:30, I got up to let the dog out—it could be that the dog is the major problem in all this—and there, in the kitchen on our soon-to-be-back-in-style green linoleum, was a 3-foot-long snake casually sprawled out.

It wasn't real big but was pretty long. Judging from its dark brown color and non-triangular head (and lack of red and yellow stripes), it wasn't venomous. I woke up the daughter; after weeks of ribbing, she reveled in the fact that she hadn't hallucinated the event.

The snake sat there placidly. With the video camera running, I got what I considered an official snake removal device—an old VCR box—and figured I'd shoo it in there and toss it outside. We like snakes; they eat rats, a big plus in the country.

But the snake had other ideas. It slithered behind the trash compactor. These days, about as many people use a trash compactor as a Betamax. This seemed like a good time to get rid of the R2D2-looking computer since we had to move it anyway for the snake. So, I pulled it out.

The snake coiled up, pretty perturbed that we had uncovered its hiding place. With a hoe—the Bride's idea of an official snake removal device—we scraped it back out into the open.

But, before we could corral it, the snake slipped under the refrigerator. So, we began taking off the lower part of the ice box. (That is, once we found our "toolbox," and I use the term loosely. We apparently have 18 Phillips head screwdrivers, a ball-peen hammer, one Allen wrench, and some skinny nails—everything remarkably rusty.)

Anyway, I got out all the fridge screws but one. Which I had to hammer off using a screwdriver as a chisel and only slightly smashing a knuckle in the process. The snake had coiled up on the motor, perhaps impressed with our persistence but most likely preferring just to be left alone.

A screwdriver urged it out. (Man, screwdrivers are handy!) We pinned the snake down, and I was ready to make a Crocodile Hunter snatch-it-behind-the-head move when it got loose again! We were quickly running out of appliances for it to escape to, but it still managed to get to the dishwasher.

Well, much of it did. I grabbed it by the tail as it got about halfway in.

So, in the dead of night, I'm in the kitchen in my underwear, flip-flops, and work gloves (all only slightly rusty) holding on to the bottom part of a snake. That's when the thunderbolt struck: So, it's come to this—*I'm a hillbilly!*

The snake and I stayed stalemated for a few minutes. Then I uttered the dreaded words, "Hey! I've got a college degree! I'm the human here! I'm smarter than a snake!" So, I began gently pulling to remove him.

The snake gave zero ground. I continued my pressure, steadily trying to draw him out. He was budging very little. Finally … a bit more pulling … it was giving some … and … the snake … tore right in half!

Some innards hung out of my half and blood dripped from the inside the dishwasher onto the green floor. I haven't barfed since the spring of 1978—wine, cheeseburgers, and the backseat of a Camaro are a bad mix—but that record was in jeopardy for a spell there.

The daughter screamed, the Bride—no fan of gore—staggered back to a chair, and I sat down on the linoleum with half a snake. At last, the VCR box came in handy as I tossed the partial reptile—still whipping about—into my official snake removal device.

Now what? The snake answered that, zipping back out of the dishwasher, intent on finding its detached part.

This time, the Crocodile Hunter move worked, and I took the now 1.5-foot-long snake, still quite active, outside. I dropped him in the grass; it was still moving about friskily and might survive, I thought.

Still, I wanted to give it every chance—the poor guy deserved a break—so, when I decided it was a bit too close to a fire ant mound, I picked the snake up again.

It bit me! The Bride found this especially hilarious since I did the official hillbilly dance of flinging it off my gloved hand and racing back into the house, flipping and flopping madly.

I hope the snake lived. But, if it's plotting revenge, I understand. I just hope next time it doesn't crawl behind the truck transmission we keep in the bathtub—I don't have nearly enough screwdrivers to move that thing.

*This was the first of three incidents that emboldened me to pull out the stops when column writing and just go for it. Actually, this wasn't a column; during the summer, the newspaper had little sports to report on, so I would write travel stories, often themed. This one in the summer of 2001 was a series about visiting various water sources in Texas. I was very worried that this column was simply too silly. However, it got a great response, and I was relieved that many others liked weird, offbeat tales, too. This was written July 6, 2001.*

# Spooky History Can't Stop Bold Creek Walkers

We were up the creek without a paddle. Or any drinking water. Or, most importantly, it was becoming quickly apparent, a flashlight.

Plus, we were trudging up Nightmare Creek.

Actually, the Bride and I were walking along South Rocky Creek near our childhood homes at Lake Whitney. But, with its strange history, it should be called Nightmare Creek. It was getting dark, and we were far from the truck.

### Strange goings-on

This creek area has a history of weirdness.

Tales of a giant bird that flies at dusk, sweeping down on vehicles and leaving claw marks on roofs, have been told for decades. Such a big bird just ain't normal.

Then there was the giant snake that was found dead along the roadside a couple of years ago. Some mighty python, at least 20 feet long, had croaked on the dusty road. Such a monster snake was certainly not normal around here.

As a teenager, I saw something late one night while driving home from work. A bright light dropped down from the sky about 3 a.m., eased over a limestone cliff, and slipped silently around the bend of South Rocky Creek. A flying saucer certainly.

That surely ain't normal.

Leaving for the creek walk, we were told one final thing: "Watch out for the boar hogs."

As a mature adult, I suddenly mentally assembled the evidence that I could not as a teenager: South Rocky Creek was actually a home base for UFOs whose occupants performed bizarre animal experiments that created monsters.

Giant birds, super snakes, and now mutant hogs. Could it now be the time for human experiments? Perhaps, but we were determined to continue this series on water in Texas. So, even, though it was 7:45 p.m., and we were armed with only a camera, we climbed the fence near the highway and dropped down into Nightmare Creek.

## Into the water

Water flowed freely just under the overpass, rolling over an old car tire from a vehicle that could've crashed after seeing something he/she shouldn't have.

While we planned to hike toward the lake, I wanted to venture around the bend the other way where I had seen the eerie light disappear so long ago. We got close, but the creek got deep as the flow almost stopped between the thick woods and high, rocky cliffs; the water's surface was covered with a slimy substance we didn't dare touch.

Those crafty aliens!

So, we backtracked under the overpass and began our trek the other way—toward the lake.

Where it flowed, the water was clear and cool. Small gravel beds were spiked with greenery as the stream bobbed and weaved along. Around the first bend, the water rose to shin deep as minnows darted about.

The footing on the limestone bottom afforded decent traction—which could be needed if mutants, either those created here or visiting from space (or both), attacked. Quickly, all traffic noise was gone, and we were amongst ... *them*.

### Discoveries

Ghostly holes, resembling the black eyes and gaping mouths of Spielbergian aliens like those from *Close Encounters of the Third Kind*, were carved from the limestone high overhead. The uneducated would say the ghoulish holes were created from years of erosion, but I now knew better.

It was yet another piece of the extraterrestrial puzzle; they were certainly some kind of detailed symbols that acted as a landing strip, directing spacecraft to this area. Either that or some really tall drunks carved them.

The sun kept sinking as we waded along. We scaled a barbed-wire fence strung over the creek. Now quick escape was impossible; the landowner was probably in cahoots with the aliens just like in that *X-Files* episode.

A grisly sight came next. In the shallow water near the bank, the remains of a snake floated. It could've been just a shed skin, but I'm pretty sure it was the end result of an experiment, much like a cattle mutilation—but smaller.

Knee-deep in water, we passed the evil-eyed cliffs and rounded the next turn. Up ahead on the right stood a startling vision right out of *The Blair Witch Project*. High in a tree was a cryptic structure symbolic of this terrifying stretch of the creek.

10

The poor Bride thought it was a deer blind, but everyone knows how tricky aliens are. It was surely a technologically advanced observation post disguised as a blind.

## Eggs from space!

It was getting downright dark now, the sun well below the treeline. We continued on, walking steadily away from our truck, with no flashlight. The plan was to reach the next bridge then walk back along the dirt road to the truck.

We would never see that bridge.

More alien carnage soon arrived. On a small gravel wash lay a turtle who was but a shell of its former self. All its innards were gone.

Yet, bouncing gently along on the creek bottom were two queer white objects—eggs!

Who knows what crazed DNA merge had taken place? Perhaps some super-intelligent turtles were housed in those eggs. Emboldened by hours of listening to Art Bell, I picked an egg up.

It was soft, pliable. The egg was about the size of a silver dollar and thinner in the middle. With good light, the mystery creature inside might have been visible; however, it was too dark now.

Perhaps we doomed mankind, but we put the two eggs back into the gentle creek water.

## Another monster

The creek kept bending and turning. The sun was almost completely gone as we pushed on toward our goal, a second, distant bridge.

Suddenly, up ahead, a gigantic form raced across the landscape above us. It was a freakishly large deer. Even in the dim light, I could see it was armed with antlers that

11

resembled a train's cow catcher. It bounded away, trying to draw us farther on. Certainly, it was trying to lure us to the alien's lair.

No way, deer! We veered off.

The creek widened on a turn and became impassable without swimming and would've been so even in the daylight. We took a side creek, but that route was closed off by trees that had been leveled by the tornado of 2000. Anyone who has seen *Close Encounters* knows that aliens can control the weather, so whipping up that storm was nothing for them.

They think of everything!

We had to face it—darkness had arrived. We were without any kind of light and could not retrace our steps without one. Our only hope was to pass through the wilderness to the west where the dirt road was somewhere in the distance.

### It's alive!

Negotiating knee-high grass in monster-infested terrain in the dark is no fun. Every noise certainly heralded the arrival of the mutant hogs or perhaps another freakish snake. Or the aliens themselves.

A half-moon tried to give us some light, but the aliens sent clouds to cover it. We pressed on, waiting for death by hogs or a visitation from outer space beings. My dilemma of course was to figure out how to run through the woods in the dark should an assault begin.

If an attack came, I was sure I could out-run the Bride. She *was* a state high jump champ, but that probably wouldn't help her much out here. I was faster than her, so I had that going for me. But it might look bad in the papers.

So, I decided I'd stay and protect her, fighting off whatever horror arrived while she tried to escape, figuring I could claim it was an anniversary present if we survived.

## Inland shocker!

We fought our way west as weeds and who-knows-what-else clung and dragged at our legs. Killer cactus blocked our way often, forcing us off our straight-line effort.

Then, we burst out of the woods into a wide clearing. This area was much brighter—a powdery white—and perfectly devoid of vegetation. Had we stumbled on a remote spacecraft landing area?

Either that or something else of great concern—a massive crop circle! How many cows had suffered unspeakable horrors here?

The Bride claimed it was an old gravel pit, but with my multi-dimensional comprehension firing on all cylinders now, I knew we were perilously close to something horrible.

Naturally, one word came to mind: probe. Everyone knows aliens probe humans and probing is almost never comfortable.

I could only hope Homer was right in that *Simpsons* episode where he got abducted by aliens only to have them say, "We have reached the limits of what probing can tell us."

Please be those aliens!

We skirted the crop circle and pushed through more brush and cedars. Leg scratchings, spider's webs (how big of an arachnid could aliens create?), and the looming, ever-present cactus made the nocturnal going tough.

Then we heard a noise. I waited for the feared blinding white light heralding a UFO arrival, and soon it came. Yet, not from above but from the side. It was a car on the dirt road just ahead.

We had outwitted the aliens!

**Safe?**

We scrambled over the fence and walked down the middle of the road back toward the truck. Still, I cautiously eyed the area knowing full well the killer freak-hogs could bolt out of the thick terrain and eventually overtake us.

Pressing on, we had over half a mile to get back to the truck. Scanning the sky for lights and listening intently for pursuing monsters, we walked quickly. And there it was at last—the truck!

Only I spied something white embedded in the passenger's door—a gigantic, white hog tusk the size of an elephant's! Ha! Not really!

Actually, we got back with no problem. Turning the ignition, I noticed it was much later than I thought. Had we lost some time we couldn't account for?

And what was that new bump on the back of my neck?

*Wouldn't it be funny if we really did cast a $1 trillion coin as was once governmentally proposed (tongue-in-cheek, hopefully, but it's politics, so ...)? I thought the idea of a change jug in the White House was funny and just went from there. This was written Jan. 16, 2013.*

# Hey, Buddy: Can You Spare a $1 Trillion Coin?

There's an episode of *The Simpsons* where evil Mr. Burns comes into the possession of a $1 trillion bill. (He was supposed to deliver the bill—with Harry Truman on it giving the thumbs up and OK sign—to help rebuild post-World II Europe. Mr. Burns kept it; eventually, Castro stole it.)

A trillion-dollar bill is absurd; a trillion dollar *coin* makes much more sense. There's a thought of legislating the creation of a trillion-dollar coin to ease our gigantic budget woes. Already, Zimbabwe has a *$100* trillion bill; you can get five of them for $2.99 on eBay. (Just make sure it isn't an African prince who is happy to cut you in on part of his inheritance if you will send him your bank account number to make a deposit.)

Of course, the American trillion-dollar coin would be worth, well, maybe not a trillion but more than Zimbabwe's (right now).

Striking a coin seems to be a crazy way to pull ourselves out of the U.S.' endless debt woes, but at least we'd quit hearing about how terrible things are right now.

The big question is: Who will keep the coin?

Will it be thrown in the White House change jug, along with quarters, pennies and those pesky Canadian nickels?

Will President Obama keep it in his pants pockets for safe keeping?

Should a conspiracy theorist put it in a weather-proof PVC pipe and bury it in his backyard with his 10,000 rounds of ammunition and survivalist vacuum-packed, freeze-dried prunes?

Certainly, they should not give the coin to me:

ME: (*at a Coke machine*) Man, I'm thirsty for a Coke.

BRIDE: Just make sure you're not using the trillion-dollar coin.

ME: Well, it's the only cash I've got on me.

BRIDE: You don't need a Coke anyway. You should be drinking only water.

ME: (*who quit listening after "You don't need ..."*) It says here the machine gives change.

BRIDE: You know what they say: Once you break a trillion-dollar coin, you end up spending it all.

The idea of this monster coin puts the last time big money amounts were minted—all bills, in 1934—to shame. Back then, the top of the scale was a mere $100,000.

The government also fired off $500, $1,000, $5,000, and $10,000 bills. That's when convenience stores all over America began the policy of "No bill over $10,000 accepted."

Finally, whose visage should be put on the $1 trillion coin? It's quite an honor. Woodrow Wilson was on the rare $100,000 bill. He took great joy stopping at the local 7-Eleven and saying, "One Slim Jim, please. And, by the way, can you change a $100,000 bill?" Then he'd take off running, laughing.

Shouldn't President Obama be on the coin? Lots of presidents and well-known politicians are already on currency; well, all the presidents are if you count the $1 coin series, but that's cheating.

William McKinley is on the $500 bill, Grover Cleveland on the $1,000, James Madison on the $5,000, and Salmon P. Chase on the $10,000.

Maybe we should have a national lottery. The winner would have his/her likeness cast and would be immortalized forever.

MAN: (*on a summer's day in 2015*) Fetch me a Coke, boy!

BOY: Uh. Grandpa, this is a $1 trillion coin.

MAN: I know what it is! I'm on it! Just fetch me a Coke, boy!

And the recession of 2016 begins.


Mark K. Campbell is the editor of this paper and gave away $2 bills at Christmas.

*The first time I saw a food truck was in Austin where they had a bunch of them lined up on South Congress Street. The concept spread and soon they were everywhere, serving all sorts of foods. It made me wonder why in the world people were so intent on buying things from out of a truck when there was a real restaurant right across the street where you didn't have to sit on a rickety picnic table to eat. This was written Aug. 14, 2013.*

# The History of Food Trucks in Three Playlets

Some things you just don't see coming.

I never imagined tattoos. On girls.

Or facial piercings. On anyone.

Bottled water.

Five-dollar coffees.

People who pay big money to buy jeans that are already ripped.

As curious as these were/are, the weirdest of all the things that I never thought would become popular—but somehow did—is food trucks.

Some guy drives up and parks this previously condemned pile of junk, throws open the side, and says he's selling Thai food.

Or cupcakes.

Or soup.

Soup! Out of a truck!

In former generations, two kinds of trucks contained food—the ice cream man and some scraggly dude piloting one that arrived around noon at whatever construction site or warehouse you happened to work at.

Now that I have grandchildren, I again pursue ice cream trucks.

You might not know this, but a dime will no longer buy a Popcicle. It takes a bunch of them.

It goes like this:

ME: (*aghast*) Does that say $2.95 for a Popsicle?!

ICE CREAM MAN: Yes. They're on sale.

GRANDCHILD: I want a Mario ice cream cookie sandwich.

ME: (*reading*) Six bucks!

ICE CREAM MAN: Not on sale.

GRANDCHILD: Poppy, just use your card thingie.

ICE CREAM MAN: Ten percent surcharge to use a card thingie.

GRANDCHILD: I love you, Poppy!

ME: (*sighs, hands over card*)

The conversation is different with the "roach coach" and its metallic flaps that open and feed rugged construction workers/warehousemen working too far from a place to get real food.

ME: What you got?

SCRAGGLY DUDE: The usual.

ME: And that's ...?

SCRAGGLY DUDE: I'm not sure. Everything's wrapped in foil.

ME: Was it made today?

SCRAGGLY DUDE: Possibly.

ME: (*aghast again*) You don't know?!

SCRAGGLY DUDE: You want something or not?

ME: I guess. (*pointing*) That one.

SCRAGGLY DUDE: Oh, man, not that one.

Today, there are exotic food trucks, some manned by supposed gourmet chefs. Who could possibly know what goes on inside a food truck?

CHEF: Welcome to my gourmet soup truck!

ME: Soup … from a truck …

CHEF: I know, right?! I left the classiest French restaurant for this. I've broken the ties of the *bourgeoisie*!

ME: (*rolling eyes*) Yeah, they're jerks. Well, you showed them. Selling soup out of a truck.

CHEF: *Oui!* That's why I named my truck Let Them Eat Soup. I serve over 50 kinds.

ME: (*under breath*) So stupid! (*sighing*) How about some chicken noodle?

CHEF: (*recoiling*) For real?! Dang! I have some with truffles and unicorn horn and that's your pick out of 50 soups? *Cinquante!*

ME: Please don't *cracher* in it.

CHEF: *Trop en retard*!

ME: I knew that was going to bite me in the *derriere*.

Mark K. Campbell is the editor of this paper, and here's the French/English translation: *bourgeoisie*: working class exploiters; *oui*: yes; *cinquante:* fifty; *cracher*: spit; *trop en retard*: too late; *derriere:* butt.

*A guy once told me this was the funniest thing he ever read which is what every writer wants to hear (if it's supposed to be funny, that is). It was an early example of writing in a stream-of-consciousness style where I didn't worry about how silly/stupid it was. This was written July 7, 2005.*

# Let's Face It: Critters Hate Us and Want to Kill Us

Did you see that television story where they're hauling in giant sharks off the Texas coast? And did you hear about the guys who lived among bears for years until one day they decided to eat them? (The bears ate the people, I mean. It's a movie out right now, *Grizzly Man*.)

Sharks and bears don't like us, apparently. Now, I know what you're thinking: How cool it would be to see a shark and bear fight each other! That'd be awesome!

As a staunch anti-bear person—my premonition of death involves bears and February which means I guess that on Valentine's Day, I'll tumble down a cliff into a bear den loaded with newborn cubs protected by a savage mama bear and all very hungry (hibernating and all)—I'd root for a shark. But a bear, being evil and all, would probably just hurl the shark onto the land and tear it up up there.

There is a reason why we humans live in houses and animals live outside. We're supposed to be separated. I'm pretty sure the genesis of that truism is in the Bible somewhere.

I have a friend who is a hunter, and he says that God gave us "dominion" over all the animals. So, he shoots a bunch of them every year with his Winchester Dominion

12 gauge. But, alas, he harvests no bears or sharks—just deer, quail, and the occasional armadillo when the deer and quail are hiding or exhausted.

(You can find just about anything on the Internet. I came upon a site that said some people believe that all animals were vegetarians back in the Garden of Eden! Because, for a while there, there was no death. However, I'm pretty sure sharks and bears weren't vegetarians. And what about the concept of a vegetarian shark?! Please! Would it attack seaweed? Kelp? Fake veggie burger patties sailed off offshore drilling rigs? It's a very complex question that we've obviously wasted enough time on.)

Let's suppose, for some crazy reason, you leave your air-conditioned home over which you have total dominion (unless you have a teenager) and venture into the wilderness. And there—wouldn't you know it!—is a gigantic bear between you and your air-conditioned car. And it's a-comin' at you! (The bear, not the car—even though that would be handy about that time.) What should you do?

A normal person would, of course, run. But, since you've decided to commune with nature, you are not normal. You surely know what to do: play dead.

Naturally, after a while, you won't have to pretend that you're dead since you will be. But, sometimes, a bear will only seriously maim someone and leave them barely alive for his dastardly cohorts, the wolves and the buzzards and the fire ants.

Now, to escape from a shark requires a different method. A good start is to stay in a boat—preferably one bigger than the vessel in *Jaws*. And air-conditioned. Or remaining on land usually works.

But, you might be swimming in the gulf, perhaps caught in one of its numerous riptides that you've gotten yourself free from when—wouldn't you know it!—a shark chomps on you.

There are many signs to be aware of when looking for sharks in the water: fins above the surface; surfboards bitten in half floating about; scary music. Two out of three of those is a very bad sign.

The trick to getting away from a shark—provided you haven't wasted all your energy screaming underwater—is to jab at its eyes. Since you'll be whaling away in every direction at the beast anyway—and you'll be whaling away underwater which means you'll be whaling in slow-motion—you might get lucky and poke it in the eye. Sharks hate that; well, who wouldn't that bother? Hmm, maybe a fly—still they have lots of eyes and could spare a few.

So, let's review:

Bears: Bad. Play dead if attacked.

Sharks: Also bad. Poke in eyes if you have any fingers left.

Flies: Lots of eyes. Smash with swatter.

The best plan to avoid being attacked by animals is to stay home. And turn down the air.

*This was a public service column that I hoped I could make funny while working in a slew of facts about men and breast cancer. It was a new adventure for me. Hopefully, other men (and women) got some chuckles and information at the same time. This was written August 26, 2004.*

# Me and My Mammogram: What? Me Worry?

This conversation occurred recently at home between me and my young adult daughter:

ME: Hey! Want to go have a mammogram with your old man?

HER: (*face distorted in look of horror*): No! Gross!

ME: We never do anything together anymore.

Back in the last century, I was a dedicated weightlifter. For about four years, I pushed those suckers around. Then, like everybody else, I quit.

A few years later (1994, to be exact), I noticed a lump on the right side of my chest. Back then, I got annual physicals and I mentioned it to the doctor; every year, he agreed with my diagnosis—probably scar tissue from weightlifting.

The doctor eventually said I should have it checked just to be sure because men can get breast cancer. So, I got it checked.

Every year, 1,500 men get diagnosed with it and 400 die from breast cancer. Even though the odds are 1-in-1,000—4-in-1,000 if you have a family history of it—the rates are on the rise for men.

It's probably our ever-fattening bodies that have caused the 26 percent increase over the last 25 years. The average age for men to get breast cancer is 67. I'm 48. Surely this lump was just from weightlifting.

Surely.

But a tell-tale malignant tumor sign is a hard, painless lump—and I'd had one for 10 years. Plus, pancreatic cancer killed a grandfather, and my 37-year-old brother died of stomach cancer in 1997.

So, I began the process of scheduling a mammogram. Now, I have an HMO and you know what that means: Instead of a high-tech machine, I'd encounter a gasoline-powered Boob Smasher 2000. ("Sorry, it's out of gas," I envisioned a technician saying as she sprinted out of the room while I remained in full-squash mode.) The pictures would have to be sent out to Wal-Mart for developing.

But, I needn't have worried. Once I finally convinced the HMO screener that, yes, I'm a man, and, yes, I needed a mammogram, things went well.

I had heard all the mammogram horror stories, mainly from the Bride who still has more breast tissue than me—right now, anyway. Knowing I'm not the most macho of men, she assured me I would cry like a baby when my chest flesh got compressed wafer thin. (Of course, she was preparing me for the worst so the real thing wouldn't seem so bad.)

At the clinic, the technician told me I was a rare male subject. But she was a pro, lining me up next to this tall, white machine (that was not gasoline powered) while I told her that a few years ago—okay, 15—my rock-hard chest would've shattered the two pieces of glass she was currently squishing my now-gravity-defeated breast tissue between. She didn't look like she believed it much.

Anyway, while the lump was on the right side, we took front and side views of each breast. True, you get mashed up pretty good, but it wasn't horrible. The pain came from getting my underarm hair pulled because of the queer positioning. Now *that* hurts.

Finished, I went across the hall and read a *Shape* magazine that said we all should be getting more Vitamin B. Then the technician came back in: "We need to take a couple more pictures."

Hmm, that didn't sound good. She showed me a spot on the x-ray and said maybe it was my nipple and that we needed to take another look. This time a got a nipple patch that would make Janet Jackson envious and had my hooters squeezed like Play-Doh into a circular cup thingie.

Then it was back across the hall where *Shape* said that Kaanapali Beach was the best stretch of sand on Maui when everyone knows it's Big Beach. Having cavorted with my chest on both beaches, I knew.

There was a knock. The technician came in with a doctor. With angulated features and a bushy mustache, the doctor looked just like the fake ones drawn in *Mad Magazine*. Is it good that he's in here? And that he looks like that? I thought they just mailed you the results.

"You look okay," he said. We concurred that my lump probably *was* just scar tissue left over from my meathead weightlifting days.

He advised me to keep an eye on it and if there were any changes to return.

So, right now I'm apparently breast cancer free. What? Me worry? No, me educated … and vigilant.

*There was much hubbub everywhere about the tenth anniversary of 9/11. Being a career firefighter, I thought I had a different perspective on the attack than others. This column references another from 2002. This was written Sept. 8, 2011.*

# Ten Years After:
# I'd Love to Change the World

Naturally, everyone is writing about 9/11 this week. I'm no different.

Back on that fateful day, I was still an Arlington firefighter. Everyone can remember where they were that terrible Tuesday morning—it's one of those startling incidents that gets seared into your memory. (Other titanic events I can recall where I was at when they happened: Elvis Presley dying [working in a pharmacy] and the two space shuttle disasters [working at Target for *Challenger* and being awaken in bed by a boom for *Columbia*]).

My journal from Sept. 11, 2001 records plenty, immediately and afterward. I was just stepping into the shower after listening to Hal Jay on WBAP say that they would be back with more information on the plane that hit the World Trade Center when the Bride jerked the bathroom door open and said a second plane had hit, a big one.

Tuesdays were and are press days, and the paper comes out no matter what. We were so busy that I ran with a column already written; the next week I wrote about 9/11. Reading it today, I'm a bit disappointed with it even though I stand by my feeling that we should've gotten right back to playing professional games. But it's not that column that sticks in my mind; it's the one I wrote a year later.

The next day, Sept. 12, 2001, I reported to the fire station. We cancelled all scheduled activities, wondering, like everyone else, what could possibly happen next. In my journal, I wrote the longest entry I've ever recorded so far in its 1,142 handwritten, legal-size pages.

On Wednesday, 9/12, we still feared that tens of thousands were dead: *"40,000 people worked at each tower, and it was almost work starting time."*

Not including the firefighters which, as you can imagine, hit home with those of us manning engines then. We knew that we would've done the same thing our brothers and sisters and other emergency personnel did, race into that building without a second thought—there was no way those towers could fall.

*"NYC has asked for 6,000 body bags, but the early estimates are 20-30,000 dead." "The debris is simply incredible. Today [9/12], more buildings fell; one 47 stories, and a multi-story hotel, a Hyatt." "The terrible visuals are forever burned into our brains."*

Major league baseball was cancelled; so was Division I football and the NFL. Air travel was stopped, skyscrapers evacuated, and Disney World closed. Americans bought flags and gave blood. Churches were standing room only. The stock market tumbled, and, early on, gas prices were jacked up, but a government edict forced them back down. The Movie Man could not find a multiplex open on 9/11.

Slowly, things improved; high school football was played that Friday—the National Day of Prayer—and never were there more patriotic crowds as Azle beat Red Oak 28-0 in the Hornet home opener.

I handled my emotions okay initially, despite the mayhem and destruction, the deaths and horror on TV around the clock. But then: *"I managed not to cry until last night when a film clip was assembled of other countries weeping and praying for America. At the changing of the guard in England, their band played* "The Star-Spangled Banner"*—that was too much."* I sat on the edge of the bed in front of our dinky bedroom TV and cried and cried.

Time mercifully passed, even if it took forever for the traumatic first anniversary to come and go. A year later, Sept. 11, 2002, I wrote about 9/11.

I had gotten off work at the fire hall at 6 a.m. and was at my usual running place, the bike trails in Fort Worth off Bryant Irvin, by 7. I ran, carefully monitoring my watch and Walkman for the upcoming national moment of silence.

I was listening to The Ticket—where morning host George Dunham famously inadvertently spoke during the silence—and the time came to pause; I was at 39 minutes, 59 seconds on my watch when I knelt on that limestone trail. It was warm and humid, a "bad" air day: *"The sun was a gigantic orange ball as it rose from downtown Fort Worth."*

Sweat poured off me as I prayed. The moment ended and I stood; next to me was an older African-American guy I saw all the time on the trails, rising to put his white cap back on his sweaty bald head.

We simply nodded at each other and went back to our business, like everyone else.

29

*It almost never fails that something weird pops up to write about. And the ol' religious figure on food/trees/shingles is a classic go-to. But this one was even crazier than usual, and I tried to take it to a goofier level. This was written Dec. 2, 2004.*

# Sacred Sandwiches and Other Edible Miracles

Can we all agree that the world is a pretty weird place?

We must, if there's to be any understanding of a cheese sandwich adorned with the likeness of the Virgin Mary fetching $28,000.

I'm not here to harp on religion. I'm the last guy in the world qualified to do that. After all, I'm no Madonna (the singer, who is Jewish this week). Like most people, I'm simply a member of the same sect as my parents, Baptist. While we're "all JESUS all the time," Catholics have scores and scores of saints and rosaries and whatnot. And a Pope. Well, Baptists do have Billy Graham ...

I've only had two experiences with the Catholic Church.

One: A few years ago, we walked over to Juarez, Mexico from El Paso and got asked to leave a lovely church because I was wearing shorts (since God had made it a million degrees outside that day).

Two: I was in a Catholic wedding a while back. It involved way too much up and down, solidifying my Baptist beliefs.

Remember last year when a carp shouted apocalyptic warnings in Hebrew to a couple of guys in a

New York City fish market? A friend and I had regular debates about this fish story.

I contended that it seemed curious that God would communicate through a soon-to-be-slaughtered rough fish. But my friend said, "I refuse to put any kind of parameters on God."

(That statement always wins a religious argument. But why a carp? Why not a nice Lake Fork black bass or even an alligator gar? That'd be a cool sight! "The end is near!" it would drawl or twang [I'm assuming it would have some kind of Texas accent] snapping its long, toothy mouth. Then the apocalypse would arrive for shrimp and perch as the blessed gar would swim over and go eat all the bait off a trotline.)

Anyway, I thought that carp story was really the wildest until the cheese sandwich tale came out. Ten years ago, a Florida lady bit into what we would call cheese toast at our house. After that solitary bite, she spied a likeness of the Virgin Mary on the bread. She quit eating, put the sandwich in a plastic box with some cotton balls, and kept it by her bedside.

A decade later, she put it up for sale on eBay, which thought it was a gag for a while and removed it from its listings. But when it was proved to be a bona fide item, an online casino bought it for $28,000. (Which, you might be shocked to know, is selling t-shirts bearing likenesses of the sandwich for $19.99.)

The biggest question I have is: Why in the world didn't the cotton ball company buy the sacred sandwich?! Their product (well, and God, of course) kept a sandwich from molding for 10 years! I'd buy those balls in a New York minute.

It looks to me like there's a market out there for food that resembles people. Especially sporting figures where devotees will drop big money in an instant to get a reproduction of their heroes.

Taking this into consideration, I carefully examined my Thanksgiving dinner and discovered the following:

- a piece of broccoli that looked like Kareem Abdul-Jabbar
- Bob Lilly's visage atop the green bean casserole
- Juan Gonzalez in a mincemeat pie
- a Cheeto that resembled Joe Theismann's leg when it broke on *Monday Night Football*
- a yam that appeared to mirror Tom Landry (with Fedora!)
- a cathead biscuit that looked like Nolan Ryan

Truly, these were amazing discoveries. But, like the NYC carp guys, these one-of-a-kind unique entities were eaten—even though it killed me to consume Nolan Ryan.

However, I must add, he was sinfully delicious!

*My car-crazy friends don't understand how I can go so long without constantly tinkering with my vehicles. (What a scam the 3,000-mile oil change edict is!) The tag at the end of the piece ended up being sort of true—it was the last time I was asked to pray at the National Day of Prayer. This was written May 1, 2014.*

# Secrets to Getting the Most Out of Your Vehicle

I'm not really a car guy.

For me, a serpentine belt might actually be a real serpent, for all I know.

Yet, I manage to get some fantastic mileage out of my vehicles. It never fails to mystify my friends who spend hours tightening thingies under the hood and fretting about changing their oil every 3,000 miles.

On April 26, my trusty 2004 Chevy Silverado turned over to 300,000 miles.

That day, I posted on Facebook: "In 10 minutes, something is going to happen to me that has occurred only one other time in my almost 58 years on this planet." That, of course, was a straight line that many cyber-comedians could not pass up, inviting jabs like "Say something witty?" and "Tithe?"

Anyway, the big event occurred almost exactly 10 years after we bought the truck. So, I average around 30,000 miles annually. (On *this* vehicle—we go tens of thousands of miles in the other one, too.)

The pickup is the second vehicle I've owned to reach the 300,000 pinnacle. A 1996 Plymouth Voyager went 340,000-plus. Then I gave it away; it might still be going.

So, perhaps you're wondering: How does a non-car guy get such amazing distance from his vehicles? With such an astonishing resume, this seems like a good time to pass on my time-proven methods.

**1.  When you hear a noise, turn up the radio.**

This has worked for me a thousand times.  AC/DC works best, but you can get a lot of mileage out of an Allman Brothers endless jam. However, Celine Dion will not work—your weird engine noise is preferred.

**2.  Click past all those annoying dashboard "messages" like "change the oil" and "you appear to be totally out of transmission fluid."**

Vehicles apparently are filled with all sort of fluids. And lot of folks are constantly changing them out. It's been my experience that doing so will not only cost you money but will quickly lead to having read all the *Cosmopolitan* magazines in the waiting room. Some people still change their own fluids, thereby saving about 85 cents. It's more economical to just wait until you literally can't wipe the thick oil off the dipstick— that's about every 35,000 miles.

**3. Fuel up only when necessary.**

The ding of the fuel low level indicator is just a challenge, really. Some say you can get "gunk" into your "fuel pump" when you let your tank get too low. Personally, I try to go as long as possible on a tank of gas. More than once, I have put 24.6 gallons in my 24-gallon tank. You might not be the sort to live on the edge like me, but I'm not about to let a dinging light boss me around! You might as well have an aired-up spare in your trunk too, you spineless jellyfish! Besides, the more you stop your vehicle, the more likely it won't restart. That's just common sense.

**4. Say nice things to your vehicle.**

Some people lavish their praise on, say, their "fur babies" when they should be lauding their car. Good luck figuring out how to get home riding on the back of Fifi (unless she is a Great Pyrenees—then maybe). No, you should be saying sweet nothings to your Ford. It's the one thing that is going to return you home through the snowstorm or provide limited protection should a bear attack.

Well, that's it. Good luck on achieving 300,000 miles. See you on the "Highway to Hell."

Mark K. Campbell is the editor of this paper and wrestled with ending with an AC/DC song since he's supposed to take part in the National Day of Prayer May 1. Oh, well.

*My mother, Veda Lois Campbell, slowly failed mentally and physically, from dementia to Alzheimer's. This was a tough visit; however, I knew many readers could relate, and several said they did. This was written May 15, 2013; Mom would die three years later from the disease.*

# A New Mom's Day

Mother's Days are different now.

We got the code to get into the locked area of the Alzheimer's nursing center—the nurse said she loved Mom—and went back.

Mom, in her wheelchair, was talking with two other women in the hallway. There's no telling what that conversation sounded like.

I said, "Hi, Mom." Her gray hair was cut very short which was okay because most times she will not allow the home's hairdresser—or anyone else—to touch her head. When they got a chance, I guess they went short.

She smiled big and said, "That's my son." That made me smile. Even though it would be the only time she'd recognize me and her calling my name was not going to happen again, it was still an unexpected bonus.

Next, she thought the Bride was her own mother. We slowly made our way to Mom's room. She was getting pretty good at tooling around in her wheelchair with just her feet.

In the room, I sat in the recliner that I had bought for dad only days before he died in June 2006. For Mom, we had purchased some artificial flowers because she would likely destroy real ones. Mom likes to tear things into little pieces.

In any event, flowers almost certainly would not stay long in her room, anyway. It took a while to get used to residents stealing each other's stuff. We've learned that that's a fact of life, so it's wise to not bring anything of value when we visit.

Some of Mom's things have disappeared through the years, and she's collected a few things of her own. This time, she had a greeting card sent to another resident, a handwritten missive that detailed the wet weather from wherever it had come from.

She talked a lot, and we just listened with only an occasional "Oh, yeah" or "Uh-huh" inserted as Mom went off on a series of topics. Sometimes her face got serious, and she mentioned a long line of unrelated events punctuated with her famous "and that's the God's honest truth" then a laugh.

She looked okay. Her back was still warped with osteoporosis, but she could cock her neck and see you.

Mom said a lot of things, little of which made sense. Well, to us, at least—she was certain she was catching us up on a variety of issues.

Sometimes she would stop mid-sentence, her attention suddenly focused on a latch on the side of the chair. Or a sock. Twenty seconds later, she returned to chattering.

We rose to leave. She walked/rolled with us into the hallway back to where we initially found her. There, we said we loved her while another wheelchair-bound lady wept near the doorway. The Bride and I took her hand, and she seemed very thankful for that.

We punched our code to exit, and, outside in the brilliant sun, I was not too sad. Mom was physically okay, overall, for 85 years. She seemed content with her small world contained in a single hallway. This mental condition wasn't going to go away, so fretting about it and wondering why served no purpose.

37

But that doesn't mean I don't pray about it constantly—and that's the God's honest truth.

Mark K. Campbell is the editor of this paper and is glad his mom's still around—many aren't.

*This was published then we immediately traveled to the state journalism convention where lots of folks talked about it. It was one of the first times that I really took a chance on a non-newspaper-y subject and wrote exactly what I wanted. It made me chuckle, so I didn't change a word. This was written June 19, 2003.*

# Attack of the Man-Breasts!

Hopefully, all the children are off to church camp so we can discuss this admittedly adult topic: the man-breast.

Of course, I never thought it could happen to me. After all, I was once the skinniest person I knew!

I really wasn't aware of how bad the situation had gotten until the Bride, overflowing with Christian, Southern Baptist love, told me—*after we had been flying in a plane for seven hours!*

Naturally, I boarded the flight throwing down a stylish look—a skintight, white pullover shirt. After all, who wants to look bad in front of everyone on a sold-out plane? Might as well give the honeys something to dream about as I walked back and forth to the bathroom.

After the seventh trip (I'd had a lot of Cokes to make up for the flight being so expensive), the Bride spoke just before we landed.

HER: You might want to consider wearing another shirt next time.

ME: (*thinking perhaps a woman had nearly fainted dead away from lusting after such an unattainable specimen*) Why?

HER: It makes you look like you've got boobs.

ME: (*looking down stunned and amazed*) Whaaaa?!

I had always assumed holding in my stomach made my chest look great! I was jutting out *pecs*, not breasts! (At least from my perspective, looking down from above.)

Soon, things began to make sense. When jogging without a shirt, I often heard murmuring right after oncoming joggers had passed. I just assumed they were rightfully impressed. Now I know I was jiggling. Or, perhaps, even flopping!

The man-breast is a frightening concept. I'd ridiculed "old men" for decades for having that, well, nauseating physical feature.

How did this horrible thing happen? I know the answer, and there's a lesson to be learned discovering (for about the 10,000$^{th}$ time now) that, despite what we think when we're 20, we're not immortal. Today's actions can affect you tomorrow! (That's the man-breast moral.)

In the late '80s-early '90s, I took up weightlifting—forehead vein-popping, scream like a caveman, finger pinching by heavy plates weightlifting. I began to pump iron with such regularity that I noticed my chest getting bigger. I did inclines, declines, dumb bells, and also used machines. I got cut! Wow, I was looking good!

That feeling wasn't shared by the Bride.

HER: It hurts to lay my head on your chest now. You're too hard.

ME: (*rightfully shocked*) Isn't that like having too much starting pitching? Or being too rich? You're saying I'm too fit?!

HER: No, I'm saying you're too hard.

ME: Whaaaa?!

Despite those cruel words, I did not let her deter me from lifting. But, like everything else, time went on and weightlifting dropped by the wayside.

A downside to stopping lifting is that the mighty chest you've built up is affected by the same gravity that changes the same area on females' anatomy. But (most) guys don't wear a bra to fake people out.

Through the years, I began to sag and did not have the benefit of a Wonderbra. I eventually became the person I had mocked so long ago—I had man-breasts!

Ironically, I felt like I was 14 again and hiding my concave chest—only this time for the opposite reason!

I find it embarrassing to have a heaving bosom. A man just shouldn't have a heaving bosom!

Today, I have finally arrived at a peaceful settlement with my hooters. Short of surgery, I know I'll just have to live with them like I do my Roman nose (which is "roamin' all over my face," thank you, Bride), hairy ears, and other perhaps less than preferred physical traits.

After all, I am fearfully and wonderfully made—I'm about a 46A, I think.

*The queer idea of growing meat was a ripe subject, especially here in Texas, the Beef State. (Well, that nickname lost out to the Lone Star State, somehow.) I also got to work in jabs at the manipulative humane society ads that run in the dead of night. And the Chia Pet joke still makes me guffaw. This was written March 7, 2012.*

# Test Tube Meat, Yum!

You just *thought* you ate mystery meat in school and hospital cafeterias.

Let's face it: Scientists don't lead the most exciting of lives. Very few collect Nobel Prizes or get to holler "It's alive!" over freshly reanimated monsters made of corpses.

Mostly—if watching PBS on post-church Sunday afternoons before falling asleep has taught me anything—scientists crouch over microscopes and look at very teeny squiggly things that will either save mankind or doom it.

Somewhere, some scientist got hungry and thought: "Man, some test tube meat sure would be good about right now." Thus, it was born.

Strips of muscle are grown from cow stem cells then mashed together to make tube burgers. Soon, more elaborate meat will be offered.

The $74 billion beef industry isn't all that worried right now. After all, what sort of rootin', tootin' Texan is going to eat something that didn't come from a slaughterhouse as God intended?

But ranchers might change their minds when people at home can grow a T-bone over a cow-shaped Chia Pet.

I'm sure this is the best news PETA has gotten since those syrupy Humane Society commercials showing sad animals peering out from under Sarah McLachlan albums entered the mainstream.

Certainly, scientists won't be long in creating test tube pigs and chickens and the world will be overrun by the critters, sending PETA into hog heaven.

I like meat. A *lot*. I would have no qualms eating something whipped up in a lab. After all, who hasn't purchased a tube of ground meat you couldn't actually see? A tube! One of those sticks of meat from a supermarket with just an *illustration* of ground hamburger on the front.

I once delivered for a meat company, and I have been in the backs of restaurants; they're nightmares. If you knew what was going on behind the scenes of your favorite eatery, you'd be *begging* for a squirt of test tube meat.

Some things mankind was not meant to see and one of those is the baloney vat at a meat factory. Whatever falls on the floor goes into the baloney vat. Man, I love me some baloney sandwiches! Iffy cooking conditions haven't stopped me from wolfing down meat or whatever the current batch of baloney is made from.

There are lots of positives to test tube meat. A big chunk of humanity can be fed cheaper. Land will be freed up. Factories that spew pollution will close.

Naturally, there's a downside. Lots of people will be out of work as homemade meat takes off. Maybe Sarah McLachlan can write a song for them.

Mark K. Campbell is the editor of this paper and likes his baloney about half an inch thick.

*It's always chancy writing about anything gay—especially today, but that was true even back in early 2005. The fact that research in non-violent ways to thwart enemies went these directions made me chuckle. The column kind of veers all over the place, but I left it alone, mostly, back then. Kudos if you know the mentioned military leaders. This was written Jan. 27, 2005.*

# Gay Bomb? We Don't Need No Stinkin' Gay Bomb!

"My sister's Gay."

People I tell that to don't have the benefit of seeing that capital G and get a bit startled at such a forthright declaration.

After an appropriate pause, I'd add, "That's her name: Gay."

"Ha, ha!" some guffaw before immediately turning on their heels.

Few things will get you in hotter water than writing about gaydom. That community is better organized than PETA. When something negative is written about them you can get bombarded with emails and letters because what you put out there can rapidly be shot around the world via that faceless creature known as the internet.

One can only imagine the barrage governmental agencies are getting after the announcement that top-secret military folks were once planning a variety of non-lethal ways to win wars. Among the ideas that came out of those brainstorming session:

• a substance that would give a person severe halitosis (bad breath)

- a chemical that would attract swarms of angry bees or rats
- a substance that would make wearers ultra-sensitive to light
- a stinky chemical that could make someone smell like flatulence (dubbed the "Who? Me?" bomb, an idea that has been around since 1945)

And my favorite that takes the old 1960's mantra "Make Love, Not War" a bit too far:

- a "love bomb" — aka a "gay bomb" — an aphrodisiac that would make humans irresistible to one another, encouraging, uh, relations between like-gendered troops.

That, my friend, is thinking outside the box. Who needs a traditional bomb? Besides, they're so loud.

The idea at that 1994 Ohio think tank was to create "distasteful but non-lethal" ways to mess up another country's military. Of course, like me, you're wondering, "Wow, our economy must've been really hitting on all cylinders back then if we paid guys to sit around thinking stuff like this up!"

The top-secret meetings surely were conducted deep in the bowels of some highly secured area:

CAPT. CRUNCH: How about a bomb that makes evildoers have real bad breath?

LT. DAN: Or makes critters attack them?

MAJOR MAJOR MAJOR: Or makes 'em smell like poots?

COLONEL POTTER: Or gays them up?

GENERAL ADMISSION: Great! Good work! Let's go to lunch! I'll apply for another grant for us when we get back in three hours!

These biological weapons were actually just pondered, never realized. Or so "they" say.

Concepts such as these are surely the ultimate dream of one historically suspect group—teenagers.

TIMMY: Hey. I got a military stink bomb off eBay!

JOHNNY: Good ol' eBay!

TIMMY: I'm going to set it off during a basketball game!

JOHNNY: Oh, that's just wrong.

TIMMY: Well, I ...

JOHNNY: Set it off during a football game—there's thousands more people there!

TIMMY: Yeah! Until then, let's go play some more mind-numbing video games!

JOHNNY: Okay!

Having been in plenty of high school locker rooms, I can attest that no stink bomb will ever approach that potent stench emitted by teens, which can be found right now a few miles up the street.

I once knew a guy who smelled bad. He couldn't help it—he just emitted an unpleasant odor. Being kind, young people, we referred to him lovingly as the "Funk Monster."

We used to say he should race through enemy trenches and watch foes fall one by one, slain by the Funk Monster.

Now, the military has caught on. True, they're using a bomb instead of the Funk Monster, but the end result could be the same.

Hmm, I don't know if the Funk Monster was straight or not.

*We got a ton of mileage out of this phrase on a vacation with friends, and it's still a running joke among us. This was written Nov. 19, 2015.*

# When 'Bless Your Heart' Is Fightin' Words

Real Texans know certain things:
- How to pronounce Mexia, Burnet, Palestine, pecan, and caramel
- How to spell "ya'll" no matter what Spell Check and your English teacher says
- What "bless your heart" really means

Of course, bless your heart actually means "what an idiot!"

*Did you hear that Jimbo cut his hand while trying to fix the Weed Eater while it was still running?"* Oh, bless his heart!"

*Hey, Jackie got locked out of the house in her nightie while fetching her mail.* "Bless her heart!"

*Poor 'ol Cletus burnt his eyebrows off when he tried to light his burn pile with gasoline.* "Bless his heart!"

Clearly, you don't want your heart blessed.

The Bride and I vacationed with a longtime friend in Mexico a while back, and she had a few too many mimosas then a ton too many other prettily name drinks—by noon.

When our friend cracked her head trying to duck under a bridge while wading in a resort swimming pool, I helped her resume near-upright status, saying, "Kinda conked your noggin there, didn't you? Bless your heart."

A former Texan, she reared up: "Don't you bless my heart! Don't you *ever* bless my heart!"

Well, of course, we did just that the rest of the trip, and, later, the postcard I mailed her said only "Bless your heart!"

You can still say the phrase in church. Not that its meaning is any different, but you can get away with gossip in church with a correctly placed heart blessing.

*Did you hear that Thelma just can't get that no-good husband of hers to come to church if the Cowboys game begins at noon?* "Bless her heart!"

If there is a hierarchy of insult phrases, bless your heart ranks above them in the South, including "God love 'em but ..." and even "I'm just sayin' ..."

Like: *There are people out there, God love 'em, who, I'm just sayin', are dumb as a box of rocks, bless their hearts.*

Now, some folks—gray hair is usually involved—truly want to bless your heart in a non-insulting manner.

I know these sweet old ladies in church mean well, but, gosh, bless their hearts.

Mark K. Campbell is the editor of this paper and please don't eat *pee-cans* around him.

*Since* On Your Mark ... *was a sports column, I wrote almost exclusively about whatever was going on sports-wise at the time. But sometimes I took a shot and branched out. (It would be a few years before I just forgot about the sports part altogether.) This is the second earliest column in this book, and one of my favorites because I think I got pretty close to the nostalgia I was shooting for. This was written Aug. 5, 1993.*

# The Sea of Love

It was almost dark when we decided to swim across the lake.

We soon-to-graduate high school seniors met after school in the late spring of 1974 at the state park. We played tag and chicken (where girls rode on boys' backs and tried to drag down opponents; only 5-6, 135 pounds, I rode on stout *Susan's* back), throw rocks, and try to impress the opposite sex. Sometimes we'd hike over to the overhang to look at the bees or swing at the playground or shout down a nearby pipe. On this day, Susan and everyone else had slowly trickled away and gone home except for the two of us.

We decided to swim across the lake. As dusk fell, we entered the water near the cabins. We had no swimsuits; we swam in our shorts and t-shirts after I had hidden my wallet and keys under a rock near the water's edge.

The water was cold—it was spring after all—as we waded out until we could no longer touch the bottom. This happened to me first since she was 5-9. Ripples from our movements were the only disturbances on the water.

Having less than four-year's experience swimming, I was a bit apprehensive about this venture, but she was a lifetime swimmer, and I knew she could save me if need be. We swam slowly, in no hurry, talking as we stroked. The 73-acre lake was in the middle of the park that sat on top of a big hill. The park was hilly with a windy road that led to several cabins and a grassy area where visitors could frolic or fish. Popular in the summer, this early spring evening had only my 1966 Chevy Caprice (the "Crème Crud") in the parking lot.

Trees pushed right up to the water in many places, and a nature trail wound through the thick woods. After reaching the other side, we returned, and approached the middle of the lake. All we saw was water and sky where a crescent moon was rising. Soon, it was too dark to see any shore.

This scene is forever etched in my mind: We stopped out there, treading water in the night. We talked about our upcoming futures at different colleges; she was engaged to the mayor's son and, on a sports scholarship, was following him to Southwest Texas State University in San Marcos. I had been dumped by my girlfriend and looked forward to leaving the small-town life behind for UT-Austin.

I had always been smitten with her since we first met. She was unattainable—beautiful, tall, and blonde with an athletic build and so all-everything in sports that I joked that it took two people to carry her letter jacket, laden with patches and medals. I was short and scrawny with two meager football patches on my jacket. And no medals. Our lives were about to go into different orbits, and we'd probably never see one another again after graduating.

But I had that moment with her. Just her and me. Treading water that was now not that cold on a black spring

50

night far away from everyone in the middle of a lake. Finally, though, we swam back to shore and went home.

We graduated that May and went off to college and that appeared to be that. But in October, the phone rang in my UT dorm; she called just to see how things were going. She came up for the Texas-Arkansas football game and, then, somehow, in some mysterious way, things started happening. We started dating. Later, I bought her a cheesy $5 jade ring and gave it to her at a Chicago concert during "Colour My World." And we got married 18 years ago this month.

We still swim.

*Not mentioned in this column is that this happened during one of two times I was on the Austin running trails and saw Barack Obama. Once, he had walked right past me, smoking and talking on his cell phone (with two Secret Service men trailing closely). In this instance, I was running near a massive political rally for him, his distinctive voice bouncing around the river trails. This was written June 1, 2011.*

# That Snapping Is the 'Poetry of the Body'

In the ever-widening pantheon of things that I'd never thought I'd say, joining "Wow, gas is only $3.89 per gallon!" and "That sure was a good Jennifer Aniston movie!" (okay, no one's said the second one yet) comes this: "I'm doing yoga!" (aka "learning the poetry of the body").

In February, after being stopped in my tracks early during a jog in Austin with sudden, searing leg pain (again), I limped straight to a nearby running store where a young twentysomething female "exercise specialist" or with some other sort of similar wordage on a certificate push-pinned on a wall in a small room had me recline on a padded table.

She began to stretch me. Then, with a stifled retching sound, said, "You're the tightest person I've ever seen!" which I thought might earn me a certificate of my own—Worst Hamstrings Ever!—but did not.

Then she started a "deep tissue" massage that was so painful Jigsaw of *Saw* fame wouldn't have put anyone through it. I asked it if was supposed to hurt this much, if she was removing muscle from my left leg like a fake psychic surgeon except not fake and she said nothing but uttered a guttural noise that made me too fearful to turn around.

Eventually, she quit, and my leg then hurt a lot more than it did a few minutes prior. She gave me some exercises like stepping on and off a curb. I explained that we didn't have curbs out in the country where I lived, that I would just use that big rock I've been mowing around rather than picking up for the last 12 years. She added that I should consider trying either chiropracty or yoga.

I feel certain that I am so misaligned that if a chiropractor got hold of me, the ensuing crack would be so loud that dials on the International Space Station would spin and superheroes across the world would whip their heads about and shout in big word balloons, "Egad! Someone's in dire danger!"

So, I chose yoga because we have a video tape (yes, video tape) on it. Plus, the Bride said she'd do it with me. (We once bought bicycles to "exercise together" and her idea of bike fitness was to pedal 65 feet then stop and take pictures of flowers, trees, bugs, and/or clouds; it was the first time I'd tried to work out and my heart rate actually *decreased*.)

There was a "Beginners Lower Body" yoga tape which seemed ideal for bad legs, so we popped that in. The Bride wisely gave me plenty of room, recalling that time we took an aerobics class in the '80s and my rhythmic flailings sent fellow exercisers flying around like a barroom fight; the survivors got in great shape, however, saying their constant laughing at watching me attempting to get fit to "I Want a New Drug" had firmed up their abs.

The tape began with more warnings than a Cialis commercial. Finally, we were welcomed by a smiling woman sitting on a Miami beach. I'm pretty sure it was a woman, even though she looked like a humanoid-shaped pile of pipe cleaners with flesh stretched over them. (Then, again, have you ever seen a chunky yoga instructor?)

We began with "namaste" which apparently means "quiver" in yoga-ese. Because, after about 18 seconds of propping my 220-pound body in downward facing dog position, I began to quiver and waffle like a suspension bridge during an earthquake. Soon, I was commanded to assume such positions as "plank," "triangle," and "warrior." Glancing at the TV through sweat literally running off my face, my planks, triangles, and warriors never resembled the lady's; she was ramrod straight while my body somehow resembled the route of the Rio Grande.

(Our instructor was insanely flexible. I suspect that somewhere, high on a variety of distant New Mexican mesas, some yoga devotees have so contorted themselves that they died up there, unable to uncontort; explorers are going to find some crazy shaped skeletons one day.)

I'll be the first to admit that coordination is not my strong suit; in fact, I'm still looking for my strong suit in the closet of life. That prior platitude is just the sort we heard from the instructor who was constantly telling us to "Let your body melt into the Earth" (which in Texas seems like a bad idea between grass burrs and fire ants) and, really!, "Soften the inner corner of the eye" and "Soften the inner organs while keeping the spine straight."

This is a lot for a quivering, middle-aged man who can't even recall where he put his phone to remember. I fear the "Intermediate" tapes might intone "Let your cornea ease while constricting your duodenum as you relax your uvula into your intercostals as you ooze into the Earth's mantle. And don't waste the planet's energy by furrowing your brow while you ponder all this."

As a beginner, however, I am steadily improving. The Bride laughs a lot less now, and I use an old robe belt (that's right; I once had a robe!) to help my leg approximate straightness.

So, I am doing yoga. And I think it's helping my injury—after a 34-day layoff, I managed to run one whole mile without pain. Still, if yoga fails, I'm prepared to visit a chiropractor; Green Lantern is on standby.

Namaste, ya'll!

*A few times each year, I had an "automatic" column—Thanksgiving, high school graduation, Christmas, and Halloween. This is one of those; I just bounced around the internet collecting factoids, so they must be true. This was written Nov. 2, 2018.*

# Be the Smartest Person at Thanksgiving Again

Last year, I fed you a gravy boat full of arcane and weird facts to amaze your family during Thanksgiving dinner.

Here's how you can retain your title as the smartest person in your family—even sharper than that freshman coming home from college. Throughout the meal, issue these strange-but-true, delicious factoids:

Nicolas Cage encouraged Johnny Depp to become an actor.

The national animal of Scotland is the unicorn.

Australia has 10,000 beaches.

The first anti-smoking movement was started by the Nazis.

Pig Beach is in the Bahamas and is entirely populated by swimming pigs.

Until after World War II, lobsters were considered "the cockroaches of the ocean" and eaten only by poor people.

Hares are born with hair, but rabbits are naked and blind.

The largest pineapple ever grown—in Australia—weighed 18.25 pounds.

Over 1,000,000 Americans name their dogs as heirs in their wills.

"Almost" is the longest word in English where the letters are in alphabetical order.

Iran leads the world in gender-changing operations.

The world's biggest turtle, a leatherneck, was found in Wales; it was 100 years old, weighed 2,106 pounds, and was nine feet long.

The word "oxymoron" is an oxymoron—*oxy* means "sharp" and *moron* means "stupid."

In World War One, a huge pack of starving wolves caused opposing Germans and Russian armies to form an alliance to fight off the animals.

The bumblebee bat is the world's smallest mammal.

Coming attractions are called "trailers" because they used to be shown after the movies ended.

Most heart attacks occur on Mondays from 4 to 10 a.m.

In 2017, thirty-five people died from taking selfies.

A lion's roar can be heard five miles away and is 25 times louder than a gas-powered lawn mower.

A baby octopus is the size of a flea when born.

The first living passengers in a hot air balloon were a sheep, a duck, and a rooster in 1783.

The Twitter bird mascot has a name: Larry, after basketball legend Larry Bird.

Sense of taste is made up 80 percent by smell.

Vincent van Gogh sold only one painting while alive.

The average lifespan of a Major League baseball is seven pitches.

During your lifetime, you will spend 38 days brushing your teeth—a good idea after gorging on your Thanksgiving meal.


Mark Campbell is the editor of this paper and omitted many body function facts.

*This might be the silliest column I ever wrote (which is really saying something). I pulled out the stops and stuck in every corny food reference I could think of. It made me giggle then and now, so it made the cut for this book. This was written March 13, 2014.*

# I Love Animals,
# They're Delicious (!!)

Did you know that Thursday, March 20 is the annual "Great American Meatout Day"?

I didn't think so.

It's the 30th one, yet, like you, I've never heard of it.

The event is sponsored by FARM, the Farm Animal Rights Movement. Kudos to them for the catchy acronym, but I'm gonna pass on the 2014 Meatout.

There are all kinds of animal protection agencies around these days. PETA hogs the headlines (rimshot!), and FARM toils away in the journalistic Back Forty (rimshot again!—I'm just gonna quit saying rimshot now because much wordplay follows; I'll just insert a double exclamation point [!!]).

It sounds fishy (!!), but FARM members are working to "end the abuse of animals for food through public education and grassroots activism."

Ain't no party like a FARM Meatout party, huh?

This is another group of folks that thinks that eating a beet is better than eating beef.

They are wrong. I don't care how much cream gravy you put on a beet, an identically adorned chicken-fried steak is going to taste a whole lot better.

Now, I'll sheepishly (!!) admit that a few vegetables taste OK and some fruits, too.

But to have to live your entire existence without barbecue or a New York Strip or chicken enchiladas seems to be a waste of life and kinda cuckoo (!! [??]).

I'll admit it: I'm too chicken (!!) to be a vegetarian.

FARM members are also very concerned about raising awareness of ingesting a "non-violent, plant-based diet."

A "non-violent diet"? True, I've eaten some pretty tough round steak through the years that required some dental battles, but I've always won.

These vegetarians' website is going whole hog (!!), listing all six cities across America that issued official proclamations for Meatout Day. Dallas joins major metropolises like Kalamazoo, Michigan and Moorhead, Minnesota.

To be fair, I have eaten some fake meat products. I've been known to pig out (!!) on some frozen pseudo-chicken patties.

Also, no one really knows what's in a hot dog—the meat content is always questionable, so I'm counting it as half vegetarian.

On March 20, FARM is seeking 30,000 people to not eat meat that day, resulting in sparing the lives of 8,000 animals. For one day.

Eventually, FARM might get put in its place by PETA if the former keeps trying to horn in (!!) on the latter's publicity. PETA is the cock (!!) of the walk when it comes to animal protection, and FARM might find itself ducking (!!) out of the way and being put out to pasture (!!).

OK, I'm (well) done (!!).

Mark K. Campbell is the editor of this paper and felt it was important to detail how the cow (!!) ate the cabbage (!!)—a two-fer!

*I always loved this column. I wrote about religion a lot because people can get so touchy about it, and it's fun to rib them. In fact, an angry Mormon reader told me he sent this piece to Latter-day Saints "headquarters" where it was now "on file." Most fun was writing a song parody and summing up the column at the same time. This one's an all-time favorite. This was written May 12, 2005.*

# If Jesus Read a Sports Column, Would It Be This One?

I don't know about you, but I'm glad the Catholics finally decided on a Pope. Now TV is back to normal.

That's a pretty crazy way they've got of picking a leader; you'd think in today's youth-oriented society, they'd come up with something a little more in tune with the times. Like having a bunch of cardinals battle it out in an Xbox game like *House of Sinners*. The high score is the new Pope.

Or maybe something sporty. Have the wannabes try throwing a football through an arcing tire swing wearing a robe and that groovy Pope hat. First one to ten's the new Pope. Kids would love that!

I know we used sports to find our latest Southern Baptist pastor. The search committee couldn't decide who to choose, so we invited them all down and had a home run derby. Got a clear winner.

Let's face it: Religions are weird. When I tell someone I'm a Southern Baptist they always go, "Are you one of them groups that's snake handlin' all the time?" That's so stupid! It's impossible to find a quality snake in January.

If you're iffy on religion, you probably need to be Church of Christ. They believe they're the only ones doing it right—plus they put together some pretty good softball teams. But, even if you can't hit, you might want to join anyway because they just *might* be right. No reason to take a chance.

Of course, they don't believe in musical instruments in church. If you want to see God real fast, try sneaking a ukulele into a Church of Christ service. They'd be on you faster than you can say Nebuchadnezzar.

Maybe you like the dressy part of religion. In that case, Mormonism might be for you. Mainly for this incredibly cool fact: You get holy underwear!

(I'm not exactly a religious authority, but I talked to a Mormon guy about this once and am basing pretty much everything I know on that one conversation—well, that and the fact that my Baptist upbringing has assured me that Mormons have zero chance of getting off this planet, let alone getting their own.)

I foresee those undies being a problem for me. I'm guessing (*guessing!*) there's Latter-day Saints SUPS: Special Underpants Sunday. I know how that would work at my house:

ME: (*waking up in a panic on Special Underpants Sunday morning*) Oh, crap! Where's my holy underwear?

BRIDE: I don't know. When did you last wear them?

ME: To the Rangers game, I think.

BRIDE: I'm pretty sure you weren't supposed to do that.

What I really wonder is: What if your holy underwear is dirty? Should you still wear it? Do you wash it in holy water? Could you substitute some Joe Boxers if they had crosses on them instead of giant red lips?

61

As a Southern Baptist, I am sworn to never clap my hands or generally move at all in church except for standing for 35 consecutive minutes of worship singing, and, later at the invitational, during 18 verses of "Just As I Am"—which always makes me think of the very un-religiously Nirvana song "Come As You Are" which can't be helping me jewel-wise in heaven—or until someone finally breaks down and goes down to the altar because the Cowboys game has already started.

If the Church of Christ softball team is full, I suggest athletes become Pentecostal. In Christian love, we Baptists usually refer to them as "pew-jumpers" for their charismatic antics. There's much physical excitement in a Pentecostal church which, as a good frozen Baptist, horrifies me. There is ample leaping about which I think would do an off-season hurdler a world of good once the service hits full bore.

Well, I feel blessed now that we've intelligently discussed religion. Let's summarize to the tune of Nirvana's "Come As You Are":

*Pope, dig that hat!*
*It's way cool.*
*Could I try it on?*

*Pass me that snake.*
*It won't bite.*
*Oops, guess I was wrong.*

*My holy shorts*
*Where are they?*
*Oh, they're under the bed.*

*Pew-jumping dudes*
*Hey, look out!*
*I could set a PR.*

*I'm Baptist, and we don't have a nun.*
*No, we don't have a nun.*

*What'd Jesus do*
*If He read*
*What I wrote here today?*

*Gee, would He laugh?*
*I hope so.*
*Or I've really messed up.*

*We're all His kids and we should have some fun.*
*Yes, we should have some fun.*

*This is one of those rare columns that came out almost exactly like I wanted. People related—who hasn't been affected by cancer?—and it won multiple awards, including nationally. It's one of the times where I really liked what I had penned. This was written July 24, 2014.*

# Here's Why We Didn't Go Home the Other Day

"Don't go home," she said.

The Bride and I were standing with a friend at the elevators on the 19th floor of one of the buildings of MD Anderson's massive cancer care complex.

We stopped by the Houston high-rise to visit a couple who both are fighting cancer. This time it was the husband in a cruel contest with pancreatic cancer, and now, liver. His just-completed procedure had left him unable to eat and depressed.

The Bride and I tried to cheer him up and stayed an hour, swapping stories about the Texas coast. Born nearby, he talked about places he loved to eat at—something that he might not be able to do with much enjoyment anymore.

Afterward, his wife walked us to the elevators. The Bride and I were trying to decide whether to make the long trek back home to the usual responsibilities that are always there or to cruise on down to nearby Galveston.

Our friend smiled with bright but clearly weary eyes, what little hair she had managed to keep from her most recent treatment wrapped in a black do-rag.

"Don't go home."

So, we didn't. I booked a seawall hotel at the last moment that ended up costing almost as much as my first car. I didn't care; after our visit, money didn't seem that big a deal just then.

In Galveston, we hopped a shuttle and ventured to a packed restaurant on the bay. I ordered exactly what I wanted instead of buying down to something more reasonable. I got a giant slab of red snapper that was perfect. I was sure the man we had just left hooked up to multiple IV bags would've loved it.

The next morning, I got up and prepared to jog. It had just rained, and it was phenomenally humid.

I spoke to a passing woman, her hair plastered down, who had just finished her run. I asked if it was "a tad humid"—she said this kind of weather needed a new word for humid.

The temperature was 80 degrees with 93 percent humidity. And the sun was coming up. The outdoor exercise rule of thumb is to add the temperature and humidity and if the total is more than 150, you should reduce your effort by 15 percent.

That morning, the number was a whopping 173—in 20,000 miles of running, I'd never exercised with a figure that high.

I took off, padding along the seawall. The ocean was a bit riled by the storm that had eventually come ashore; early morning surfers were delighted to have bigger-than-normal waves to mount.

I got tired fast. At the turnaround, I dropped down to the beach and ran on the packed sand, an occasional wave from the incoming tide reaching my shoes.

Soon, I was exhausted. I stopped and walked a while, looked at the waves, the surfers, the kids playing in the sand amid the seaweed, and the awakening resort town.

There was no way I was not going to finish this run—not after what I had seen the day before. It's corny to "run for somebody," but that's what I did that moist morning.

I made it back to my starting point, a wooden arch marking the one-time site of the Balenese Room, a sparse remnant of days now long, long gone. When I'd finished, completely sweat drenched, I waded into the ocean, the endless waves soothing my weary legs, then out to the breakers to just stand for a while.

Afterward, the Bride and I lounged down at the elaborate pool, the water perfectly cool, surrounded by healthy, well-to-do folks booked into this "luxe" hotel.

Good for them, I thought. And, our hospitalized friends would say that, too.

We could never run with this ritzy hotel crowd, but that wasn't the point. Life's about living, well. Today, that was at this snazzy resort.

Thomas Wolfe wrote that you can't go home again.

And sometimes, you shouldn't.

Mark K. Campbell is the editor of this paper, and he paid $14 for two English muffins and a Coke at the fancy-schmancy hotel.

*There was plenty of hubbub when it looked like Hillary Clinton was set to win the 2016 election. Conservative radio talks shows were aghast and far right folks were sure that things were about to go downhill fast. This was fodder enough, not to mention that there were actually some good tips in the magazine I read. This was written April 22, 2015.*

# What to Stash in Case the Survivalists Are Right

Let's say the extremists end up being right: That, when Hillary Clinton is elected president, all our guns will be confiscated, and the United States will be given over to ISIS. Or zombies.

Only those survivalists who weren't in bed with the Illuminati or who wisely never paid federal income tax will possess the items needed to exist in a post-apocalyptic America.

The other day, while the Bride was shopping for a Weed Eater at Lowe's, I was eating a hot dog and reading a magazine up near the registers. There, an article detailed just what those lucky enough to not die after the end of America as we know it will need to continue to live.

You might want to start hoarding these items:

- Big dogs—one more level of protection
- Duct tape—duh
- Manual can openers and mixers—you'd hate to waste ammo blowing off the top of some Del Monte peas

- Coffee and tea—scrambling to live in a dystopian world is not the time you want to ween yourself off caffeine
- Hard copies of medical and gardening guides—a nuclear blast might mess up Dr. Oz's internet site
- "personal care" items—toilet paper and feminine hygiene products might be highly valuable a couple of months in (this also includes condoms and birth control options; reproducing right off the bat is probably not wise)
- Insulated ice chests—not for keeping things cold (there won't be any ice) but for keeping items from getting frozen
- Bolts, nails, glue—little things will mean a lot
- An inflatable mattress—maybe the most valuable futuristic item; your spouse is not going to like sleeping on pine needles for long, and if Mama ain't happy …
- Seeds—after all the dandelions and mushrooms and canned goods are consumed, somebody's going to have to grow some real food
- Bleach—not for coloring your hair since no one will care that you are a fake blond anymore; the bleach is for purifying water
- Washboards and clothespins—your old high-dollar, front-loading washer will have zero value
- Baking soda—for putting out fires since you'd never waste precious water on flames
- Booze and cigarettes—great for trading with hillbillies

- Reading glasses—not much use having the *How to Grow Anything* series if you can't read the books
- Scissors and sewing supplies—when racing through forests in fear of your life, you'll likely eventually tear your shirt or pants
- Nail clippers, soap, wet wipes—you may never shower again; why survive if you die from being nasty
- Bicycles—it's unlikely that, even in pre-apocalyptic today, that giant pothole on Highway 199 is ever going to get repaired, so, when under attack, you can ride and out-distance some guy on foot trying to catch you while he's loaded down with all those "personal care" items

Mark K. Campbell is the editor of this paper and almost certainly will go down in the first wave.

*I wrote of lot of quiz columns like this one. There's a correct answer that is almost always obvious, but the real fun was coming up with a bunch of jokey ones—and maybe a few options where that weird answer could actually be right. This was written May 18, 2017.*

# Are You Uncouth?
# Take the Etiquette Quiz

Once upon a time, there were rules society followed, proper guidelines that proved to everyone that you were not a hillbilly, but you could, in fact, host a dinner party or eat before others with the proper utensils.

I am old enough to know that a male never offers to shake a lady's hand unless she extends it first. And that a man takes his hat off when entering a building.

I came upon a 1987 *Emily Post on Entertaining* book at an estate sale and these answers were culled from it.

Here's a quiz to see how you'd do in high-falutin' company:

1. Can butter plates be placed on the table in formal dining?
   a. Yes
   b. No
   c. An I Can't Believe It's Not Butter plastic tub is okay if there aren't too many toast crumbs in it
2. Who is served first in formal dining?
   a. The host
   b. The lady of honor on the host's right
   c. The fat guy
3. How should one eat oysters on the half shell?
   a. Cut them

b. In one bite
c. Don't, they're gross
4. Can you ask for seconds at a formal dinner party?
   a. Yes
   b. The hostess will decide when/if you need seconds
   c. No, especially if they're oysters
5. Who pours at an informal tea?
   a. The hostess
   b. Someone the hostess has arranged in advance
   c. It's every man for himself
6. When giving a party in someone's honor, when does that person appear?
   a. First
   b. Last
   c. When it's time to make a beer run
7. Should one bring food to a dinner party?
   a. Never
   b. Maybe, if it's really good
   c. As long as it's not too-long expired
8. How long should dinner be delayed for a late guest?
   a. 15 minutes
   b. 30 minutes
   c. Until the backup pizza arrives
9. How does a host end a party?
   a. "One last nightcap."
   b. "Here's your doggy bag."
   c. "Get out, moochers!"
10. Can I invite my boss to dinner?
    a. Never, only the boss can invite you—then only to a social lunch

      b.  Yes, especially if you survived the latest budget cuts

      c.  Are you crazy?!

11. How far in advance should party invitations be issued?

      a.  A month

      b.  Two to three weeks

      c.  Whenever you finally buy some stamps

12. Must one give a reason for declining an invitation?

      a.  No

      b.  Yes

      c.  Yes, if it involves "sorry, that's when the Cowboys game is on"

13. When men guests find their place cards at a formal table, do they sit down immediately?

      a.  Yes, to avoid crowding

      b.  No, all the women must be seated first, then the hostess

      c.  Only if they're at the "kids' table"

14. Are husbands and wives seated together at dinner parties?

      a.  Yes

      b.  No

      c.  Are you crazy?!

15. How do I talk to my hostess' servants who are serving?

a.  Never speak to them

b.  "Is it fun being a servant?"

c.  Ask only if they know the score to the Cowboys game

ANSWERS: 1) a; 2) b; 3) b; 4) b; 5) b; 6) a; 7) a; 8) a; 9) a; 10) a; 11) b; 12) a; 13) b; 14) b; 15) a

Mark K. Campbell is the editor of this paper and will surely stain his shirt with something that won't wash out before the night is over.

*This is another column that won multiple awards—back when you could approach the gay subject without getting savaged by all things PC. It's a true story. The Seinfeldian final line was more in the public mind back in '05 than it is today, of course. This was written March 17, 2005.*

# Having a Gay Old Time Answering Questions at Home

Do I look gay to you?

In 1974 when I was a senior in high school, my wonderful, kind mother asked if I was gay—a question I would, incredibly, hear again later in life.

Actually, the word "gay" wasn't exactly in vogue for non-heterosexuals back then, and my mom didn't use "gay" but I caught her drift. And I was flabbergasted.

"No!" I shrieked (which is a bad thing to do if you're trying to avoid looking stereotypically gay). "Mom, I'm on the football team!" Back then, that was enough to qualify you for straightness because everyone knew that no gay dude could ever play a sport—especially football. "Why in the world would you ask that?!"

The fact that I had had few (female) dates and that, aside from working after school, I generally just hung out at home most of the time made her wonder, I guess. (This was B.C.—Before Computers—when young folks actually went outside occasionally.)

I assured my mom that I was not gay, that I just didn't have much to choose from—*females* to choose from—in the Podunk town where I went to school.

"Well, I was just wondering," Mom said.

Somebody else was, too, about 31 years later.

I came home from another hard day of recording local history in a newspaper format when I was met at the door with, "Are you gay?"

Now, three decades later, lesbian chic has come and gone, the metrosexual fad has faded, and the bloom is certainly off *Will and Grace*. Gay now means gay—not happy or jolly but un-straight.

The fact that my Bride of 29 years asked me this question made it even more perplexing. Naturally, the first thing I said was, "Have you been talking to my mother?"

You would think that if anyone could vouch for my preferences, it would be the human I reproduced with. However, that was before Oprah became involved.

The Bride had been watching an episode where married men were coming forward confessing that they had had numerous affairs with like-appendaged persons. Hundreds of affairs, for years and years. I was not one of those men.

"Why in the world would you ask me that?!" I shrieked.

"Well, on *Oprah*, all these guys were married yet cheated on their wives with other guys."

I said, "I can't even find the time to mow the yard; who has any kind of time to have an affair?"

She chuckled, "Oh, I was just kidding—even if you did work in the fire department and spend 22 years sleeping in the same room with a bunch of burly guys."

"Gross," I re-shrieked. "If I was gay, I wouldn't match up with some kind of gorilla firefighter! Give me a little credit!"

"Well, I was just wondering," the Bride said.

Good 'ol Oprah. Don't get me wrong: I love Oprah. She's gotten people reading again, she's funny, she's generous, and she's the most powerful woman in America, maybe the world.

If I was ever on a talk show, I'd choose hers. Maybe I'd get a car or be on the one where she gives everyone all those presents, Oprah's Favorite Things. Every audience member gets a slew of gifts that are shown onstage by Oprah. When they announce that this audience has been lucky enough to be the one to arrive for Oprah's Favorite Things, the crowd is required to scream non-stop for an hour.

Okay, listening to that much screaming over blenders and cashmere sweaters might *turn* me gay. But otherwise, Mom and Bride, I'm still straight—not that there's anything wrong with that.

*Growing up in Texas, all our jokes were Aggie jokes. This column is a bunch of them written at one sitting one afternoon. The concept was so bizarre—an A&M university branch in Israel. It was football season, and, since everything is all-football in the Lone Star State in October, I also made up a schedule for A&M-I to play. This was written Oct. 30, 2013.*

# Greatest Aggie Joke Ever? How 'bout Texas A&M-Israel?!

OK, look: I'm a UT Longhorn, and I was thoroughly indoctrinated to believe that Texas A&M students were the ones who couldn't cut it elsewhere.

I know they are good at planting stuff and yelling at football games—usually because they were losing—while they stand up all the time then reach over and hug whomever is next to them, regardless of gender.

Now, one of A&M's distinguished alumni—Gov. Rick Perry (who has had lots of people yelling at him for all the years he's been governor)—is proposing building a Texas A&M in Israel.

Yes, *that* Israel!

And you thought West Texas A&M was out in the boonies.

Of course, most Aggies are already easily confused, and plenty already read right to left. Making a real campus over there seems, well, like an Aggie joke.

So many questions ...

Who in the world would Texas A&M-Israel play in football?

Do you want to play at Syria?

Would Kuwait be the Southlake Carroll of the conference where all those rich kids have already spent years in specialized football camps?

Isn't Qatar a great choice for an A&M-I Homecoming foe?

When you're at a TAMU-I game, do you really want to stand around all those guys yelling in Hebrew for four quarters? Oy!

What happens when the A&M-I star quarterback autographs a bunch of yarmulkes and starts hawking them all over the Middle East?

It might also be hard to schedule games over there with all those Jewish holidays; no one's going to play on Yom Kippur.

Since the A&M fight song is so focused on another school—UT-Austin—will the Texas A&M-I fight song be all about Egypt? Do you know how hard that would be to rhyme? (On the plus side, the "Aggie War Hymn" already contains words that could be straight out of the Dead Sea Scrolls: "Chig-gar-roo-gara-rem.")

Do you really want a bunch of Aggies that close to a tension-filled part of the globe? ("Caneck"—another mystery word in the A&M fight song—might mean something very different over there.)

Can you imagine a hillbilly Aggie giving directions in Israel? "Uh, yeah, head down to Giv'atayim then hook a left at Modi'in-Maccabim-Re'ut—you can't miss it. If you hit Kafr Qasim, you've gone too far."

What if Aggies wander too close to holy relics? While the A&M-I campus is planned for Nazareth, Jerusalem is right down the road. What if an Aggie tries to ride his dirt bike through the Mount of Olives or spray paints "Beat Sudan!" on the Western Wall?

And how long will it take for an Aggie angler to figure out that he's not going to catch a black bass out of the Dead Sea?

Yes, these are pressing questions that will require giant brain power to work out, people of major aptitude like those who created the Affordable Care Act web site. (When Kathleen Sebelius, Health and Human Services Secretary, toured Texas trying to find someone—anyone!—who had successfully logged on to Obamacare, even Aggies told her, "Keep on moving, lady.")

If Texas A&M-Israel becomes a reality, Gov. Perry hopes it builds "bridges of peace and understanding."

But good luck getting a room at the inn when A&M-I hosts Qatar.

TENTATIVE SCHEDULE

| | |
|---|---|
| Aug. 30 | at Turkey |
| Sept. 6 | Middle Tenn. State |
| Sept. 13 | at Sudan |
| Sept. 20 | ^ BYE |
| Sept. 27 | * Iraq |
| Oct. 4 | * at Iran |
| Oct. 11 | * at Syria |
| Oct. 18 | ** Qatar |
| Oct. 25 | * Kuwait |
| Nov. 1 | * at Oman |
| Nov. 8 | * at Egypt |

^ Yom Kippur
*Middle East Conference
** Homecoming

Mark K. Campbell is the editor of this paper, and he almost deleted this column three times.

*When my little brother died at 37 on June 17, 1997, I wanted to fashion a column that was memorable, so I pondered it a while. I stuck in a device that, upon reflection, really wasn't necessary: every sentence has at least one word that begins with 'F' in it. My boss always said he liked this column. It won several awards and was one of three straight American Cancer Society Texas Media Award honors earned—plaudits I'd just as soon never been given. It's a good recollection of Mike's life, I think. It was written Sept. 18, 1997.*

# One Life ...

Frankly, this is a column that has filtered through my mind for several weeks—formless sometimes, taking flight other times. For, after all, how do you recount a life in this tiny rectangle? I feel I must try.

My little brother, Michael (Mike) Ellis Campbell, died June 17, his body eventually faltering from a relentless stomach cancer. Frail, he barely resembled the robust, fit man he was a couple of years before.

Funny, everything he loved seemed to begin with an 'F': freedom, football, fireworks, fun.

If anyone ever lived a full life in 37 years, it was Mike. Not that it was always the kind of life others should try to forge for themselves.

When young, we played football, among other sports, constantly. Pass and catch, fake and go. We painted cheap helmets with cheap paint, fashioning them after college or pro teams. The future was far away, then.

But teenage years come frightfully fast. Soon, the figurative fork in the road appears and decisions must be made. I went for college, marriage, children. Mike fell into the ferocious, frenzied world of drugs in high school, a foray

80

that dogged him for years. It caused our relationship to fragment.

Living a frenetic life, he finally got caught in his self-created maelstrom and went to prison. Now, those who feel people can't be rehabilitated are wrong; Mike saw the light when he saw years with no more fishing, football, or freedom. When he was freed, he stayed out.

He found a wife, adopted a Hispanic daughter, and loved working at his job at Georgetown's Sun City. The world felt right again. He was an expert fisherman and knew where to fish at Lake Whitney and around Port Arthur on the coast. We all gathered at Christmastime again and our family was reassembled. Families forget faults; it seemed feasible that we'd spend decades together.

But a stomach pain in late 1995 wouldn't go away, and Mike felt feeble with a fire in his belly. He went to a doctor and got the fearful news: stomach cancer—only liver cancer is worse, we were informed.

Like a flood, the disease advanced over him. So, surgery was followed by chemotherapy and radiation, "treatments" that fatigued him tremendously. His once mighty body failed before our eyes.

We managed a fishing trip to the coast right after the removal of most of his stomach. But, we all knew the odds, that 95 percent of stomach cancer victims don't live two years beyond their surgery, and the fire in his gut eventually returned.

If cancer has any possible benefit, it's that victims have time to get their affairs in order, make sure that things are fixed right, and Mike did that. After he found peace and that final phone call came, we cremated him in Austin. He wanted his ashes—which are not really ashes at all but grit, like fine gravel—spread in Lake Whitney, and we did so one warm August morn.

Around midnight the night before, down on the lake's bank where Mike had set up his tent a hundred times, we fished. On the radio, Lynyrd Skynyrd's "Freebird" came on. We cranked it, the song bouncing off the limestone cliffs; guitar heavy, it felt like the right song for him.

Mike refurbished guitars, and I got one afterward— it's over in the bedroom corner, and on the glossy, black Fender are his fingerprints, still.

Farewell.

*Sometimes a topic pops up that begs to be written about. Like gay ducks. This was possibly tricky territory, but I dove in full-bore with, for some reason,* The Simpsons *in mind. Word play options were many, and I didn't pass on them. Of all the columns I reread for this collection, this one made me laugh often again. This was written March 12, 2009.*

# If It Walks Like a Duck and Talks Like a Duck, It Must Be Gay

Ducks are gay! I knew it!

It's obvious some ducks prefer an alternative lifestyle—I mean just take a gander at the garish wood duck—but it's been officially declared that there's a bevy of gay ducks out there.

That was the verdict of a story in *Scientific American* that has sent shock waves through a variety of communities from late night talk show hosts to Ducks Unlimited where decisions on what to wear to the organization's annual prom are now in question.

Poor Cherry. A female blue duck in England, she is the last of her kind; male blue ducks Ben and Jerry want nothing to do with her.

CHERRY: Hey, hottie dudes!

BEN: I'm gay.

JERRY: Me, too.

CHERRY: Oh, great.

BEN: Maybe you should hook up with a swan.

CHERRY: Ewww, that's sick!

If there is no way for ducks to reproduce, how long until there will be no ducks at all? If I know my Charles

Darwin and his wacky theory of evolution, it could happen in, say, a few million years.

And, if I know my *Baptist Standard* and Young Earth proponents, then we'll be duckless by next January.

And if I know my Hollywood movies, then the gaudiest ducks are probably the gayest—either that or lonely cowboys or politicians.

Let's face it: A mud duck is too plain and dumpy to be gay. But a Baikal duck is *clearly* gay.

This gay duck revelation has reverberated all the way to Washington where politicians are goosing the national stimulus package with funding requests to study indigenous wildlife in their respective states.

For instance, a senator from North Dakota got $370 million to examine male pattern baldness in the great American bison. Seven jobs are expected to be created by this bold venture that is generating icicles of Hope in that frozen-solid state.

For the record, while I am straight, I have not only owned a duck but eaten one. I couldn't tell if it was gay or not. It *was* greasy.

It's too early to tell how the killing of gay ducks will affect hunters:

JIM BOB: (*early morning, crouched by a pond*) Ya'll know if there's a limit on gay ducks?

BILLY WAYNE: Just shoot!

JIM BOB: You know, I don't feel right about shooting a gay duck.

BILLY WAYNE: Shoot!

JIM BOB: (*lowering gun*) Billy Wayne, you sure look pretty in this early morning light.

BILLY WAYNE: Oh, crap. I guess I should've figured you out from that rainbow camouflage.

Actually, there are over 1,500 species of critters that display "homosexual behavior" according to another article in *Scientific American*—clearly a leading gay publication—like baboons, penguins, and garter snakes. While I seldom see baboons or penguins on the trail I run on, I frequently witness entwined garter snakes. I always assumed they were just wrestling.

Clearly, things are way gayer on the planet than I thought.

Anyway, let's review:

Ducks—gay

Late night talk show hosts—gay

*Scientific American*—gay

*Baptist Standard*—gay

Hollywood—gay

National stimulus package—gay

First name of *Honor Thy Father* author Talese—Gay

North Dakota—gay

Jim Bob—gay

My sister—Gay

That Saturday morning TV commercial aimed at kids that says not to say things are "gay" because it could hurt someone's feelings—gay

Being in a merry, lively mood—gay

Writing a column about gay ducks—double gay

Trying to break the *Guinness World Book* record for most times using "gay" in a column—gay

Well, that's about it and ... oh, no! A bright light and weird noise just like on *Lost*—I've been "flashed forward" and am time traveling into the future to my answering machine next week:

*Beep!*—Yeah, this is Charles Darwin VI. Prepare to hear from my lawyer.

*Beep!*—*Baptist Standard* here. Ditto.

*Beep!*—This is Hollywood. Expect a Scientologist on your doorstep soon.

*Beep!*—This is Congressman Bud Wiser from North Dakota. Don't you ever come up here! We'll stampede you with a herd of majestic and iconic, if slightly balding, American bison!

*Beep!*—Yeah, Mark, this is Pastor Van. I'm gonna need to see you in my office. And bring your deacon name badge.

*Beep!*—*Guinness World Book* recordkeeper Reginald Worchester Wellington calling. You missed the "most times using the word 'gay' in a column" by three. Sorry, old chap.

Next week: cross dressing armadillos.

*I waited for the primary people referenced in these two columns to die before writing the pieces. I think they're the sort other families can relate to—everyone has some weird, hilarious story in their generational histories. I always got a lot of mileage telling these tales in person and was glad to finally record the incidents for prosperity. This first one was written June 5, 2014.*

# Here's One of Two Terribly Wonderful Stories

People occasionally come up to me and say that they feel like they know me after reading this column each week. I think that's a nice compliment, but the Bride ... well, not so much sometimes since I occasionally reveal something weird that has happened to me/us that she'd as soon stay private. (Like snakes in dishwashers and whizzing on poison ivy to kill it.)

Sorry, pumpkin, this is one of those columns.

Actually, this is one of two of those columns that I have set aside for decades; now, after 1,126 prior On Your Mark ...s and 22 years, here's the first one.

It's really a terribly wonderful story of true love. Kinda.

First, some background: I grew up in a family that wasn't exactly independently wealthy. We lived off the Weatherford Traffic Circle in Fort Worth with a bunch of other families that were generously called middle class.

Still, I had a phenomenal childhood, full of baseball and sunshine and baloney sandwiches and Kool-Aid and bikes for Christmas (that I found out half a century later my dad went into cruel debt to get for my little brother and me).

My mom was a child of the Depression. She threw away *nothing*. She also proved that anything could be wrapped in foil—it's the female duct tape. When we moved her to an assisted living apartment a few years ago, we went through drawers and found an astounding number of things wrapped in foil then put into a Zip-Lock then wrapped in foil again! And it would be a button or bookmark.

Anyway, the point is that, because of her Depression upbringing, we never threw *anything* away at our house.

The Bride found this out early in our marriage.

Visiting, we had just finished eating supper—I'm sure Mom made me something special, something different from everybody else because, well, I'm special (a trait the Bride did not smile upon, by the way)—when the Bride volunteered to wipe off the table.

She got tossed a rag from the rag drawer. The Bride didn't think much of the cloth at first. Yeah, it was kind of raggedy but would do the job.

Then she noticed what it was: an old pair of male underwear, probably mine from several years prior.

I had spent my entire life cleaning off tables with underwear. Who hadn't?

Sure, the tighty-whities were no longer suitable for their original purpose—which, admittedly, had lasted way longer than their usual life expectancy—but, despite its holiness, they cleaned off a dining room table just fine.

Here's the true love part: The (terrified) Bride went about cleaning, non-judgmental and smiling. (Afterward, however, she washed her hands for 35 minutes.)

You must really love someone to use their old underwear on a dining room table and not make a federal case out of it.

This concludes the first of two terribly wonderful stories.

The second is a Thanksgiving tale and will arrive Nov. 25.

Mark K. Campbell is the editor of this paper and these days his worn underwear mysteriously disappears.

*Likely, every family has an instance like this—when something is so funny but laughing would be highly inappropriate. I waited a long time to write this because I didn't want to embarrass anyone. It's lore in our family now. And, it's probably one of the times I laughed hardest in my life. This was written Nov. 25, 2014.*

# The Second of Two Terribly Wonderful Stories

Back in June, I detailed the terrible yet wonderful story of being a newlywed and the Bride offering to clean off the table after a meal with my folks.

My Depression Era parents threw nothing away, so the cloth the Bride was tossed was my old discarded teenage underwear. The fact that she never flinched while swabbing away with those disintegrating tighty-whities was a tribute to her love.

Last June, I promised a second terribly wonderful story, one that would arrive at Thanksgiving. This is that incident.

It was Thanksgiving Day 2000-something. Turkey Day is the big holiday in the Bride's family. Everybody heads to her parents' house, additional leaves are inserted into the long table, and a gigantic amount of food is displayed for consumption.

For some reason, I'm usually the guy to issue the pre-meal prayer even though I'm famous for not going on too long while heads are bowed. (Maybe that's why I'm chosen—so we can get to the food faster.)

Anyway, there we were in 2000-something, the clan returned home, and all gathered about a steaming bounty. It was time to offer the prayer of thanksgiving.

Only this time, I wasn't the speaker. The Bride's elderly aunt was asked to pray. Now, Auntie was an angel— a sweet, kind, gentle soul who died earlier this year after a cruel, lengthy decline from Alzheimer's. (This incident occurred before the disease's onset.)

We all held hands. And Auntie began—I assume.

Because what came out was unintelligible. Overcome with emotion, Auntie was emitting some sort of high-pitched voicings that sounded exactly like Beaker, the scientist assistant Muppet. (Perhaps her prayer was in tongues. But we were all Baptists and had no interpreter gifts, so I'm not sure.) The prayer went on—a squeaking that somehow kept rising and rising in scale.

Naturally, it was all I could do to not laugh. The Bride knew that and squeezed my hand with impossible spousal, don't-you-dare power. I glanced up and knew my angelic teenage daughters were also going through the same kind of silent gyrations—internal aerobics, a kind of comedic isometric dynamic tension—to avoid bursting out in guffaws. The squeaking prayer went on and on, so sincere amid the tears—and so, so funny.

This was a horrible predicament. Mercifully, the heartfelt, genuine, indecipherable prayer did finally end, and I excused myself and bolted outside. The giggles fought to escape my body as I ran for the door. I made it outside before laughing so hard that I soon had tears of my own.

I laughed so hard that my asthma kicked in.

Eventually, I said my own prayer, thankful I didn't burst out laughing at what would've been the most inopportune, *meep! meep! meep!* time imaginable.

Mark K. Campbell is the editor of this paper and would not dare recreate this incident Nov. 27 even though that would be quite the callback.

*A memorable day is often a good topic for a column, and so is one that is terrible. I hate throwing up and had gone decades not doing so until a fateful trip out into the Gulf of Mexico. This column won several awards, including my only Katy Award from the Dallas Press Club. I have not barfed since this event and hope to never do so again. This was written June 16, 2005.*

# Old Man and the Sea Score: Sea 1, Old Man 0

*Once again, we must begin with a warning: This column is mostly about throwing up. Since some words are so unseemly and fire off visceral responses—like "extended warranty" or "Michael Jackson"—let's refer to the 'V' word that means the body's oral rejection of previously tasty food as "clomit" for decency's sake.*

The record is over; I am no longer the Iron Man of Clomiting. It was quite a run if I say so myself. I went from May 1978 until June 11, 2005 without hurling. That's over 25 years.

I was beginning to think I was never going to spew again, making that long-ago wine/cheeseburger/screwdriver/Camaro backseat combination the final gut-wrencher. I never forgot it, a torso-torqueing disgorgement that was so full-bodied that I think I barfed up a toenail.

Through the years, I had survived numerous near-retches—a cruise, illnesses, and gorging myself like that time I ate 60 shrimp, well, just because.

As Lou Gehrig discovered (from heaven, I presume), records fall. And my clomit mark did, too—miles out in the Gulf of Mexico.

This is how the record ended:

The Bride and I decided to eat right off the bat upon our arrival at Port Aransas. We chose a hole-in-the-wall joint; aren't those always supposed to be the best, the restaurants where the locals eat? Yet, we were served some very greasy fish and shrimp. But, I ate mine. Then most of the Bride's.

Looking at the clock, we saw we could make a 3 p.m., 5-hour deep-sea fishing trip so we signed up. We disregarded the captain's warning that the gulf was "a little rough," passed on a refund, boarded, and sailed away.

We got out of our protected waters, but the cruel waves arose before we even cleared the jetty. We sat up near the bow and soon the boat was slamming into white-capping waves. Sea spray stung all, even those sitting near the back. Within minutes, everyone was drenched. The Bride decided early to retreat to the interior of the boat, mainly to protect our camera.

I hung on tough up front, along with another couple. Initially, we laughed as the boat reared up then whomped back down. But, after a few minutes, it stopped being funny. Spray after spray pelted us, as many as 10 times per minute, each one feeling like we were being slapped by stinging jellyfish tentacles.

On and on we went. I had a death grip on my benchseat, and, despite the heaving deck running with water, I thought about trying to move inside. Aside from the fact that I imagined it was like a slave ship in there—and it almost was, the Bride reported, with slick bodies (many, it must be noted, seriously overweight) wallowing over one another in sticky heat—I wasn't about to try to traverse that 20 feet.

Denying the laws of physics, waves were going in four different directions at once! We simply continued leaping waves, with half the large boat rising out of the water then crashing back down. Over and over again. And we traveled on and on, constantly getting pelted and stung by the evil sea.

After an hour and a half of this torture, we finally stopped. I felt like I had survived a death-defying accident, like the time a drunk hit us. The boat immediately began to roll back and forth, but at least we weren't getting blasted with jellyfish spray.

Zombie slaves immediately began sliding out of the boat's interior and chumming the waters with great regularity. Poor suckers, I thought. I helped a couple of teenage girls with their poles and dropped my line as well. The girl next to me immediately caught a 2-foot shark.

Then, I started feeling a bit queer. I sat down. All around me were most of the passengers on the boat who had earlier ejected their former meals. Soon, I forgot about fishing. In fact, I forgot about everything; I was a water-logged landlubber who was *way* out of his element.

I glanced at my cellphone (which, miraculously, still worked despite being submerged in my pocket). It was 5:18. Apparently, the act of calculating that we'd be on this stinkin' boat for over three more hours engaged my long-dormant clomit mechanism.

For me, there are few things worse than clomiting. I know people who almost enjoy it because "they immediately feel better." The Bride will be in the middle of a conversation, lean casually to the side to hurl, then calmly continue her sentence. Clomiting is almost like a hobby for her.

However, for me, it's a horrible, gut-rending endeavor. When I deduced that I had *three more hours* of feeling this nauseous, that old nightmare feeling of pre-clomit loading accelerated.

94

I rushed to the boat's side, and the record splashed into the gulf. It was terrible! I'm not a quiet clomiter; I sound like I'm being mugged, like I'm a Crip being bludgeoned by a gang of Bloods. Over and over I was slugged.

Like someone who literally laughs "Ha! Ha!" I am a stereotypical clomiter, one who, when making that fake clomit sound, isn't faking.

My guttural noises were ear-splitting. Heads whipped around (in Cancun, I think) and a whale leapt out of the water and glanced over with one of those giant eyes, wondering what that god-awful sound was.

The teen-age girls—who somehow were unfazed by this maelstrom—looked over in horror, and the Bride, who possesses not only awesome gams but bona fide sea legs, laughed and laughed!

That greasy lunch was gone. I'm pretty sure I ralphed up a small organ, perhaps a chunk of pancreas (I couldn't be sure), before I sat back down.

Three more hours … what an eternity that was! Finally, a million years later, land came into sight while I had endeavored to keep my mind busy to avoid a re-engagement of the spewing process.

Twenty-five years is a good run. Mathematically, that means I won't clomit again until July 2031—which is absolutely the next time I will go deep-sea fishing.

*Like many pieces here, this is a true story. A guy once told me he appreciated the coda after the column and this one especially fit, I thought. I heard back from plenty of church folks who confirmed this issue. This was written March 26, 2014.*

# Verily I Say Unto Thee: Hurry Up Already!

Uh-oh. I clearly had chugged too much sweet tea and the church small group was just beginning.

This was nothing new; church folk bring food and drink, and it gets consumed at a very unbiblical pace at times. I am highly skilled at this.

The 22-minute DVD lesson began. It was about Joseph and forgiving or something like that, but I had more pressing, restroom concerns. But, of course, it's always bad form to just get up in the middle of a church lesson, even if Max Lucado is lecturing from a TV screen.

Another problem was that I knew that there would be a discussion afterward then we'd break up into small prayer groups. More time delays ...

And—always!—within this sort of piecemeal gathering, there's somebody who is a professional, Old Testament prayer sort, full of "beseeches" and "verilys" and scads of "thees" and "thous." They are PPPs: professional prayer persons.

Some Christians are astounding at praying for "hedges of protection" and donning the "armor of God" and a slew of other groovy phrases snatched from the Good Book.

Not me.

In fact, I was recently chastised for my meal prayer—which has been the same for decades:

*Dear Lord:*

*Thank You for our safety and good fortune. Please keep watch over our family, friends, and troops. Thank You for this food. In Christ's name, Amen.*

I always felt that covered it. It's sincere and honest and keeps the hamburgers from getting cold.

(The first thing I learned in journalism was two words: Be Concise. Everything can be shorter. [Prayers are not journalism, however. Clearly.])

My just-fine prayer, I was informed by the Bride in Christian love, was perhaps a bit rote. Maybe I should mix it up a bit, I was told. Perhaps try something different occasionally.

I'm not a big out-loud prayer. When I was a kid in youth groups, I prayed silently often—imploring to not be chosen to pray aloud.

I'm fine praying orally now, even if it's a tad briefer than the pros.

Usually, it's the old folks who are PPPs, the guys and gals who sit in the back of whatever gathering is going on— the King-James-is-the-only-real-Bible people—who will whip out elongated, flowery, dense praises and laments that can go on for a while.

I have no doubt they are sincere when they bring in detailed statements concerning "discernment" for politicians and helping the evil, biased, liberal media "see the light."

Then, there's always the PPPs' standby, the weather.

How things are going outside is always a constant with the pros' prose and their confined audiences. Especially rain that's either appreciated for recent fallings—

"Verily, we thank Thou!"—or pleading for absent rain—"We beseech Thee!" (That last prayer has been going on for about three years now.)

So, anyway, after Max Lucado told us on the TV to be more forgiving, we chatted as a group for a while. I remember nothing. All those glasses of tea ...

Then came the breakout into smaller groups. Thankfully, my gang didn't have a PPP. Soon, most of the other groups had broken up and were milling about in the hallway and our group joined them (including me, after a blessed visit to another room).

But the Bride got a PPP who was on fire with a series of Old School words and phrases.

Now, there's something kinda cool about an 80-year-old person who has been a member of the same church for 70 years intoning concerns and thanks in a Shakespearian manner. There's poetry there, no doubt, and it's Spirit led, hopefully.

However, a lengthy prayer doesn't work for all of us. Just like some folks are okay with the NIV Bible or even—gasp!—The Message, we're also okay with knowing that God knows our hearts, and it might not be necessary to evoke every situation you can think of.

Still, if you need to whip out some "verilys" and "begots," go for it. I'll cut back on the tea.

Mark K. Campbell is the editor of this paper and once dared to take a Living Bible to Sunday School.

*This is the first column where I took a chance and avoided the usual format. I hoped recording my journey in the 1996 Dallas White Rock Marathon in one long paragraph—a "you are there" concept—would work. And, apparently, it did. The column was a multi-award winner. I would try unique looks regularly afterward in the paper, either changing out the On Your Mark ... photo or printing the piece upside down or sideways or, once (not reprinted in this book), all along the entire six columns of the newspaper page without a return. My boss said it was too hard to read and few would make the effort, but lots of folks did, they said. (One loyal reader said she used a ruler to keep things straight.) This was written Dec. 12, 1996.*

# Rock Run On

What a crowd! Better lie, as usual. How about a 3:15? Can't get into the street so I'll wedge in with all these others and filter in. Lady, you better move if you're not running. Man, it's cold. It's going to be murder turning into that north wind. "This ya'll's first marathon? I've run a few and my advice would be to drink, drink, drink. Every time you get a chance." Five seconds to go. Wonder why they use that crazy horn instead of a gun to start the race? All right, I've made it to the starting line—20 seconds. Not bad. Go slow. Just beat four hours. We turn right in less than a mile. Better head that direction. So far no one has fallen. Oops. That relay runner dropped his baton. Good thing someone picked it up for him. Hey, that guy has a pouch in the back of his shorts for his baton. That's a good idea. I'm still freezing, but it'll heat up, and I'll be glad later I'm not in a sweatshirt or pants. Where's Steve? Here's that wind! Ah, the first aid station. Drink. Every time. Feel OK but not as good as I thought I would. Wow, that guy's pretty big. Over 200 pounds easy. Good luck to him. Maybe I shouldn't complain about 185. Mile 3 at 25:47. Too fast. Slow down! Get back to the 9-minute pace. I'm real tired of listening to the social calendars of the two women behind me. Well, they'll leave me behind soon enough. Last time, a line of people rooting for Mexican runners was here. There they are. Whew, I'm way too weary for just six miles. Maybe I should have heeded the advice in the race packet and not run if I had been sick in the last week. But I couldn't just blow off three months of training. OK, here's the lake. I'm on pace now but feel weird. At the halfway point: 1 hour 58 minutes—two minutes ahead. Man, where are my legs? The wind off the lake is still kind of cold. Wow, those houses are amazing. Those huge, perfectly cut acres of yard go right down to the road. And those monstrous houses! Cool. Fourteen miles. I'm not going to make it under four hours. I must have gone too fast early on. Again. I'm starving! That's "Born to Run" at mile 16. I'll run at least that far. Oh, a Jolly Rancher. I hate watermelon, but I'm going to eat it. Just make it to 17. A sign: "Donuts ahead." Food! Grabbed four. I'll get another from this guy on the end. All right. The roadway. This small black lady is pretty old. She's not making a sound. I'm probably grunting enough for both of us. Just reached 20 miles. Oh, no. The next two miles are on a rise. "Free beer." I don't think so. What mile am I on? Twenty-one or 22? Where is Steve? Four is just not going to happen. Come on! Just get to 23. Now it's OK to walk. My legs, my quads are shredded. Three hours 32 minutes. If I could just manage three 9-minute miles. No way! There's that guy and girl I saw back at mile 12. They are walking too. Go! Come on! Just jog to that speed limit sign. OK. Walk one minute. That couple is running again. Stay with them. Oh, man. I *did* train, right? Mile 24. Drink one more time. Mile 25. Walk a bit. Run to that stop sign. Walk. Jog to the next intersection. "The finish line is just around the corner," a guy says. Run with that couple. Yes! There are the balloons across the finish line! Pass these four runners on the straightaway. Cross the line: 4:05:04. Walk the chute. Here's the medal. All that for this? There's Steve. He beat me. I don't care. I just want to sit down.

*This column made me chuckle as I wrote it, especially "vision-questing snakes." It's a true story, and it took several days to get the water lines cleared; the critters had entered through the wellhead. This was written Feb. 28, 2018.*

# Showering With the Enemy

I have never heard this before.

The Bride stuck her head in the bathroom while I was washing off and asked if fire ants were coming out of the shower head.

That sounded kinda bad—like a cheap horror movie—so I stepped back. (Not very far; our house was built in the 1970s before showers got big enough to park a pickup in.)

The ant pronouncement came on the heels of us earlier discovering/disrupting a couple of snakes when we were digging out a water cut-off. The duo, bullsnakes probably, was minding their own business, curled up in the dirt and awaiting springtime until we jerked the lid off their quaint abode.

We don't kill non-venomous snakes. We pick them up at arm's-length with some sort of garden tool and escort them outside the fence where they probably beat us back into the yard.

Our country "estate"—lovingly called the "Crackerbox Palace" after the George Harrison song— seems to be a beacon for snakes.

Maybe word has gotten out that, since we don't kill them on sight, the Palace is a mystical place among serpents, a venue where some sort of slithery rite-of-passage or snake walkabout can be conducted amongst the towering enemy, humans.

So, through the decades, we've had vision-questing snakes just about everywhere outside and inside the house.

Twice we've found snakes in our dishwasher.

They are in the sunroom at least once a year.

We see them freaking out and zooming away from our mower all the time.

Again, the Bride and I are snake friendly, because the critters are great vermin killers.

We kill only the venomous ones—after all, we have grandchildren.

In the Palace, we've contended with scorpions—I once got stung in the middle of the night while sleeping. We kill scorpions on sight, too. And the black widows that populate our area. Not to mention any poor spider that might have the misfortune of displaying a marking resembling a brown recluse; if it looks like it has a "fiddle" on it, we squash it.

However, for the most part, we just scoop up whatever non-human entity that has managed to somehow get into the house and toss it outside where nature takes its course and the invader immediately gets eaten.

So, for the most part, we are gentle, pacifist souls at the Crackerbox Palace—with one more exception.

Fire ants.

They are straight-up evil. We have had them short out electrical boxes and mess up our wellhead. Not to mention that just taking a stroll and looking down to see a writhing, stinging mass on your bare leg can make you dance like that time you had too many margaritas in Mexico.

So, when the Bride came in and asked if fire ants were shooting out of the shower head, I was understandably concerned.

She said she had discovered fire ants in the washer and toilet. (This was another sentence I had never heard in my lifetime.)

It's hard to imagine where the worst place to have fire ants is, but the commode could be No. 1. (Yeah, I just made the easiest of potty humor jokes.)

Now, there are tales of snakes curled up in toilet bowls and seeing that might scare the, uh, stuffing out of you, certainly.

But fire ants?! Even other ants hate fire ants.

Bathing with ants is not unheard of. We have a friend who was washing her hair when her shower began ejecting equal parts water and fire ants.

The recent February rain deluge is the likely culprit of sending fire ant hordes scurrying to safety, and they ended up in our water line.

Either that, or maybe they're in cahoots with the snakes and something really freaky is going to happen this spring at the Crackerbox Palace.

Mark K. Campbell knows the Bride always hates it when he writes about critters in the house.

*Like many men, I guessed, their spouses are on them to eat better. I like few vegetables, and, to the disdain of the Bride, I've always said that a multivitamin can replace whatever it is you're supposed to get from broccoli. When it dawned on me that I'd been taking an all-purpose vitamin for over a quarter of a century, I computed the numbers. The Howard Garrett mentioned is a local talk show host who espoused all things organic. This was written Jan. 12, 2006.*

# Analyzing a Consumer and His Consumables

Try not to get too scared, but there's about to be some math attempted shortly. Also, there's a gross anecdote below.

So, the other day, I told the Bride, that I thought I would make a good medical subject, and she whole-heartedly agreed. "Especially mentally," I assumed she mumbled.

(Here comes the gross anecdote.)

My hearing has been going because, as a kid, I was a serious ear Q-Tip/forefinger abuser. I rammed those suckers in there all during my formative lifespan. Years later, while paddling along at the bottom of a swimming pool, pressure shot a wad of wax out of my ear as big as the candy bar Bill Murray fished out of the pool in *Caddyshack*. People fled the water like that "Hey, there's a shark!" scene in *Jaws*. Amazingly, I could suddenly hear like Superman! For a while, anyway.

(End of gross anecdote)

My reasoning why I would make a good medical subject: I have ingested an incredible amount of stuff in my near-half century on Earth—I mean *a lot* of junk.

While I have been an athletic sort and fitness minded forever, I wonder if all that sporting and exercise have actually been beneficial. To use a 24-Hour Fitness cliché—"If your body's an engine, you'd better be putting good fuel in it." Well, if Butterfingers and diet Cokes and wedding cake are fuel, I'm a V-8. However, if *drinking* a V-8 is good fuel, then I'm a used Yugo.

I'm pretty sure I've done some things right. Running mile No. 18,000 will arrive around June. I ate a salad once. And, I've taken a multivitamin every day for more than 25 years.

Once, at a seminar, a nutritionist said that only dummies take multivitamins. "If you looked in a Port-A-Potty, you'd find a mess of undigested vitamins." (That sentence was so strange. First: Who looks in Port-A-Potties? [Well, once my checkbook fell into one, and, yes, I fished it out.] Secondly, did she have to use the word "mess"? It made me giggle.)

Anyway, the nutritionist obviously didn't know about my ASA—Amazing Stomach Acid. It's too bad I can't capitalize at having such potent stomach acid; it's one of the few things that I'm really good at. I could digest a shoehorn or a fishing lure. I am certain I could handle a simple tablet.

While I've popped a vitamin daily for decades, I have avoided the Substance Flavor of the Week—like creatine, fish oil, or rose hips. (The latter was just too Howard Garrett-y.)

For years and years, I gulped Centrums, mainly because they had the prettiest box. But one day, reading the soft-core magazine *Men's Health* at my doctor's office, I learned that Centrum was frowned upon because back then, those vitamins contained iron, and most men do not need additional iron in their systems. It's true I couldn't walk past a refrigerator lest I be covered in those bendy advertising magnets hawking pizzas and radio stations no longer in business. (Remember Memories 97.9? Q-102, Texas' Best Rock?)

So, I switched to One-A-Day Men's vitamins because the magazine said so, right after the story "Ten Tips to Being a Real Man in the Sack." Also, it had no iron. (The vitamin, not the sack.)

Through the years, I have consumed a phenomenal amount of vitamins and minerals. For me, it was much more convenient to swallow a tablet than to try to eat an eggplant, certainly the most giggled at vegetable.

(Here comes the math part.)

Figuring on 25 years, I have calculated—almost certainly incorrectly—that I have put this amount of these things in my body (allowing for an occasional missed dose caused by not having a diet Coke to wash it down with [I *really* hope aspartame ends up being okay; however, there could be a crusty chemical stalagmite ever-growing in my colon right now]):

- 121,875 mg of zinc
- 243,750 mcg of biotin (whatever that is)
- 975,000 mcg of chromium (again, whatever that is)
- 28,437,500 IU of Vitamin A (if this good ... wow! I'm doing great!)

Contrast this with consuming 410 entire wedding cakes.

It's all probably a wash.

*This was the second of two columns about a sheep that wandered up our dirt road that's three-tenths of a mile uphill from a highway. We weren't sure what to do with Tina—aside from naming her after the llama from the then-popular movie* Napoleon Dynamite. *Everything worked out nicely. This was written April 7, 2005.*

# A Happy Ending for Tina the Sheep

Last week, this space detailed the story of a lost sheep that ended up on our doorstep. We named her Tina. This is the rest of the story:

We had been unsuccessful feeding our new arrival. Because the last time I started the mower, the blade had flown off—really; it had a bent crankshaft, and the repairman said to "just throw the whole mower away"—our grass, along with a nice crop of bluebonnets and paintbrushes, was high and green.

Tina seemed to prefer grass only as a last resort, however. So, we researched online for the care and feeding of sheep. Apparently, we needed selenium which, wouldn't you know it, we were low on.

We also discovered that we needed phosphorous, copper, and corn silage—none of which we had on hand. Also: "Sheep can have access to all the corncobs they want."

Well, luckily for Tina, I had just consumed what I hoped was the non-silage part of an ear of corn I had bought at Chicken Express a few hours earlier.

I threw the corncob on the mound of food we already had piling up on the front porch for her—hard dog food, carrots, and lettuce. And not cheap iceberg lettuce, but fancy "hearts of Romaine" that comes in a package that costs $3.29 for 19 cents of lettuce.

Anyway, Tina wasn't too crazy about any of our offerings. She ate none of it.

So, a few days passed and just when we were wondering what else to throw out on the porch—already visitors had to enter on the other side of the house now—the county animal control truck arrived to fetch Tina.

The skinny Animal Fetching Lady had come alone, so I offered to help her catch Tina. I had just run a few miles and hadn't showered yet so why not snag a sheep?

Tina smelled a rat right off. Actually, it was probably me because she gave me a look like, "Man, you smell worse than me, and I'm a sheep!"

She cautiously eyed us. Animal Fetching Lady fetched one of those poles with a loop on the end that you see wardens in Florida catch alligators with.

We maneuvered the ever-cautious Tina into a corner and approached. She quickly spun out of our grasp a la Barry Sanders and dashed away.

The next time we surrounded her, she head faked us one way and bolted the other—a classic Emmitt Smith move. We never touched her.

Finally, we got her close to the wire fence. Tina knew she was in tight quarters. She looked a bit fearful since a giant, stinky man and a skinny woman with a noose on a stick were closing in on her.

"Can I tackle her?" I asked.

"I'm still getting over surgery from the last time I tackled something," said Animal Fetching Lady, adding, "but, they don't kick or bite."

Heck, I'll tackle anything that won't kick or bite. That's how I met the Bride. (She bites now, though.) Tina decided to try and leap over the fence, and when she

109

bounded off it like a trampoline, I pounced like Lee Roy Jordan!

I said soothing words to her which was quite a miracle, really, because when I wrapped my arms around all 40 pounds or so of her, I discovered Tina's belly was covered with a jillion grass burrs. (You may recall that our property is being used as a pilot program for the growing of mutant grass burrs.)

We got Tina to the trailer and Animal Fetching Lady drove away with her.

She surely had quite a tale to tell in the holding area. (Tina, I mean, but maybe both.)

A call from the sheep's owner completes the story. Tina was bound for processing, in her owner's trailer heading down FM 51. Apparently, even sheep know what "processing" means; *Mission: Impossible* style, she escaped en route, getting out of the trailer while it motored down the highway.

That was in mid-March. We didn't come upon Tina until late March, so she had wandered around the countryside for about two weeks.

Fortunately for Tina, her Springtown owners read last week's column and recognized her from the picture. So, she's home, certainly telling rapt livestock about the time she escaped from a truck until a stinky man grabbed her.

I'm glad she's around to tell it.

*This is the earliest column here, the thirteenth one I ever wrote. Combined with another piece two weeks later— about a friend who was seemingly inept athletically until he stood on a tee box where he miraculously became the greatest golfer I've ever seen—it brought the first recognition from my peers as the duo won a statewide award. Here, a group of slow-pitch softball players—we were the Austin Angels—drove to Houston in an RV, often harmonizing to the Commodore's "Three Times a Lady" to the dismay of many fellow travelers. This was written Nov. 5, 1992.*

# A 'Dome Lesson

Watching television the other night, I saw a replay of a great American spectacle—the pursuit of a foul ball at a major league baseball game. That much-sought-after souvenir, a reminder of the game, was yours to keep.

A guy made a nice one-handed catch on TV, and every time I see such an effort, I think of the play I had in the Astrodome in 1977.

The Astros had a mean-looking, hulk of a player named Cliff Johnson who did a turn as a Ranger later but probably had his best years as a Toronto DH.

Anyway, Johnson, a truly inept fielder, was playing leftfield, just below us. In the 'Dome, the leftfield fence is very tall (as Pete Incaviglia discovered last year), and, from the safety of my lofty perch, I began—like any true baseball fan—to terrorize Cliff Johnson.

High above him, I hollered every bad fielding insult I could conjure. Inning after inning I deluged him with iron glove insults: "What's that clanging? Oh, just Cliff pounding his glove"—that kind of sophomoric banter.

111

Finally, between outs in the middle innings, Johnson turned around and peered over the towering left field wall. At me. His glare stopped me cold, and he shook his finger in a "you're a bad boy" fashion. As the inning ended, he glanced back again as he trotted toward the dugout.

Johnson was the lead-off batter in the Astros half, and I watched—quietly—as he dug in. He smashed the first pitch, and, of all the 20,000-plus fans in the Astrodome, the baseball locked onto me like a laser. This ball had my name on it. And it was en route. Fast.

Naturally, I was not one to be intimidated by a rock-hard spheroid traveling hundreds of miles per hour. I was going to catch it and be on *This Week in Baseball*. I stood and immediately violated the first rule football coaches teach you about receiving: I decided to catch the ball against my body rather than using just my hands.

To quote the latest *Indiana Jones* movie: I chose poorly.

That missile ricocheted off my sternum before I could even get my hands up. I can only deduce that the ball went *through* my body because it landed in the seat behind me where an old man calmly bent over and picked it up.

I refused to give Cliff Johnson the luxury of me watching his home run trot. Finally, though, as he took his position in the field, I had to look up. He had the biggest Cheshire cat grin you've ever seen.

"You're the greatest fielder who ever lived," I yelled. He chuckled, nodding his head.

Later, in a McDonald's restroom on the way home, I discovered I had gotten a souvenir of the game after all. Clearly visible on my sternum were the stitches of a National League baseball.

*For some reason, this column got a lot of positive feedback. You never know when writing how something will be perceived or accepted—you just write it and send it out there. This was written Nov. 30, 2016.*

# A Family and Its Stump: It's at My Place Now

Much to my delight, the door was unlocked.

It was Thanksgiving Day, and the family was where it always was on that day—at Lake Whitney at the Bride's parents' house.

After the death of my parents, we are selling their small lake cabin with the screened-in porch perched on a high ledge with dramatic views of towering limestone cliffs across the way. We had had the place cleaned to be made presentable for sale, and it must've worked because it sold on the first day of its listing. The Realtor said we needed to get what we wanted out of the cabin before the new occupants arrived.

I just wanted one thing: the family stump.

Two grandchildren were with me, and I regaled them with tales of my teen years as we wandered around the small place. I had forgotten the key, but, thankfully, the back door was unlocked.

While the grandkids ran around the echo-y, near-empty cabin, I headed for the stump that's about 19 inches tall and 17 in diameter. I don't know where it came from. I only know I needed to save it.

That stump has been around a while, always in the exact same place in the cabin; right next to my dad's easy chair where generations often heard his motto: "Get out from in front of the TV!"

I have long memories of a variety of things being placed on the stump. There was always, without fail, a *TV Guide* perched atop there; when the digest-sized magazine expanded to full size, the symmetry of the stump arrangement was seriously imperiled. That's because it held so many other items. Like beer. My dad liked beer. *A lot.*

When, late in life, a doctor told him that all that alcohol was messing up his liver, Dad switched to non-alcoholic beer and drank just as much. That old stump has soaked up a lot of condensation from Old Milwaukee cans.

The wood chunk used to hold Dad's cigarettes (Winstons) and a lighter. Then, again late in life, that doctor—what a killjoy!—said that Dad had better quit smoking. So, he did. On the spot. For years after, a single cigarette—inside a clear, cylindrical container barely bigger than the smoke—sat on that stump alongside Dad; he never picked it up, saying it was a reminder of a vice left behind.

The stump could be ornery. It rebuffed more than one little toe, stumped on the stump.

We finally rolled it away a few feet from Dad's "Archie Bunker" chair when we bought in his hospital bed in the early summer of 2006. He died a few days later; we took the bed out and returned the stump. Then, Mom kept it busy with milk and letters and her Bible before she began her Alzheimer's descent and had to move away.

Now, it's my turn with the stump. It's out in my sunroom; it'll have an old coffee cup, *Texas Monthly*, and a Bluetooth speaker on it. It's a really good stump.

Mark Campbell is the editor of this paper and thinks the stump weighed more than its 30 pounds as he toted it a great distance to the car.

*I wrote 13 of these holiday letters through the years, and they always got a nice response. Initially, the idea was to mock the "bragging" of well-to-do folks who sent out annual holiday letters filled with their kids' accomplishments and the family's worldwide travels. But I eventually quit referencing that and just went off the cuff. By the way, we joined a group of neighbors and sued the below-mentioned motocross track—and, against great odds, we won! This was written Dec. 14, 2016.*

# The Annual Christmas Letter, Back by ~~Popular~~ Request

In an effort to give the United States Post Office workers a break while they huddle in the back room sending in online applications to FedEx, here is the annual Christmas letter of what we Campbells enjoyed/endured in 2016.

JANUARY

Because 2015 was the wettest in history, we had two family Christmas parties in January. At one, the Bride rode a Hoverboard with ease while Mark was told he was "too heavy" which he took as an insult until the thing burst into flames.

FEBRUARY

We met old friends in Austin, and, on a whim, paid more for a hotel room than Mark's first car; afterward, we had whim remorse.

MARCH

We had a nice wildflower crop which the grandchildren enjoyed sprawling in and eventually smushed into a pulp.

The Bride took up golf at a time in life when Mark had to quit because of his (literally) gnarled fingers which not only point in every compass direction but look like someone has sewn pebbles into some joints.

APRIL

In Las Vegas, we saw Elton John in concert (sadly, no "Love Lies Bleeding/Funeral for a Friend") and the Beatles "Love" where Cirque de Soleil people on bungee cords and trampolines somehow made "Being for the Benefit of Mr. Kite" even cooler.

We bought a $65 bottle of wine—whim remorse No. 2—that back home we found at Albertson's for $12.

MAY

Mark's mom died of Alzheimer's on the second. It was not a shock but not expected, either. He was glad the suffering ended for her.

A bull snake found its way into the grandkids' Disney doll play castle. Fortunately, only the Bride was playing with it at the time.

JUNE

Mark found his old draft card from 1975 and his number was 38. He's forever a Nixon fan for the president abolishing the draft soon after.

The paper did okay at the annual contest, but the big news was that Mark found $5 while running.

Mark turned 60 and had all the children and grandchildren over—which is the best present, of course. (Close behind was the $60 Pappadeaux's gift card.)

We bought a new (to us) car and again assumed a car payment for the first time in nine years—and it was just as painful as we remembered.

JULY

After a restful trip to Red River, we came home to discover that a neighbor had built a motocross track on his recently purchased property right out our front door.

AUGUST

Mark and the Bride celebrated 41 years of marriage in their time-honored tradition—working.

SEPTEMBER

Because it's what we do, the clan was all gathered, and we raced to the coast to spend a long, quick weekend at a beach hotel in Galveston. Our herd/horde was quite a loud load and not only did several employees quit, but the hotel manager was found curled up in a fetal position in the lobby as we left.

Granddaughter Jubilee got burned by a Mexican fast-food restaurant's cheese sauce. We now know the melted concoction can reach 160 degrees. It burned skin off her five-year-old chest, but after weeks of tending, she recovered just fine. Not so her mother, however, who will not return to that chain.

At the end of the month, the Bride became the loveliest 61 year old on the planet.

OCTOBER

One of the knuckles on Mark's fingers began bulging with "effusive fluid" which he pierced with a pin and squeezed out regularly which always went over big at Wendy's and church. The doctor literally recoiled when looking at his hand. She said to keep it covered which Mark does, getting a lot of mileage out of showing his ailing middle finger to others and motocross parks.

Mark bought an old school Batman suit which he thought was double groovy; the Bride thought it was "asking a lot of Spandex." Mark learned to appreciate the fact that zipping something up the back is a special skill that he struggled with because "his muscles were too big" to contort that way.

Mark's big brother Freddy died, officially of pneumonia but from liver disease, too. We had had a gathering at his Lake Whitney place after Mom's death. The final days were not pleasant for Freddy; Mark was glad the suffering ended for him.

NOVEMBER

The motocross park began attracting RVs pulling numerous bikes. It got very loud often—and that was just the Bride voicing her views on the matter.

The oldest daughter's family finally escaped Oklahoma and got back to the Great State of Texas. All grandchildren are within 10 minutes now—a great blessing.

DECEMBER

Mark again played a wise man in the church Christmas production; he remains okay with the typecasting.

The motocross neighbors cut a sewer line on their property, but, since it was a decades-old lateral line from our system, we had to pay for the repair and "hazardous" cleanup. So, the Bride is getting a septic system for someone else for Christmas. She is beyond thrilled, as you can imagine.

To raise funds, Mark is willing to don the groovy Batman suit for birthday parties and bar mitzvahs. He might need help zipping it up, though.


Mark K. Campbell is the editor of this paper and left out the part where his beloved pickup with just 337,000 miles on it died on the Interstate. (It's being fixed, however.)

*I cracked up the whole time while writing this. I headed to the internet to find euphemisms for passing gas—and, boy, there were a ton! This is another column where I was wondering if this was something that should be in a family friendly newspaper. But, I laughed when writing and rereading it back then, so I published it. It got some great feedback, almost all positive, and eventually won a few awards. Two weeks later, I followed this piece with a "pulling back the curtain" column on how the "Stink to Think" column came about. This one was written June 15, 2016, the other June 22.*

# Stink to Think:
# Loving Your Body Emissions

*It's been a long time since I've had to start a column with a disclaimer but ... some people might find the following disgusting and stupid. Oh, and it also has f-words in it.*

A "recent British study" (is there any other kind?) has shown that passing gas can be tremendously beneficial to your health—*and to that of those around you!* I don't know how these studies get done or are funded or what poor souls have to undergo the discernment and compilation of evidence, but I'm glad they did.

According to "Dr. Nandi" on Facebook—I think he's real because his profile picture shows him wearing a white medical jacket—pooting not only helps you live longer but might actually prevent dementia.

Gaseous body emissions also aid in the diminishment of cancer, heart attack, and stroke chances, apparently. So, if you truly love your family, you'll let `er rip whenever possible.

The magic bean for farts (there's that warned-about f-word that used to be verboten in civil society) is that the odor contains hydrogen sulfate.

Then comes this magical sentence from the good doctor: "Researchers believe inhaling it actually causes your brain to grow stronger and protects your brain from dementia."

Inhaling "wind" makes you smarter! Lots of people owe me decades' worth of apologies—I've been increasing folks' brain power since the `60s.

It's my understanding that every actor from the campfire scene in *Blazing Saddles* went on to become titans in academia.

Sometimes you find out things about your spouse after you're married, and the Bride discovered quickly that I could be a tad gassy at times. It's a great relief—in many ways—that after you marry you no longer have to exert control over so many body issues.

We were so poor when we first wed that passing gas was our main entertainment. (Well, I found it far more entertaining than she did.)

Throughout my lifetime, I've witnessed some historic funk—on both ends of the spectrum.

I once worked at a fire hall with a group of guys that bravely took on the challenge of keeping one another from getting dementia by literally eating the worst stuff they could imagine the night before they came on shift duty. I saw a guy once make a roomful of firefighters literally flee, one exclaiming over his shoulder, "If you're sick, go to the hospital!"

Task Force 9 should live forever!

There's another benefit from trouser trumpeting: It joins music as a world unifier. Backside ballistics are truly universal. Everyone of every race, color, creed, gender, transgender, whatever emits their own personal hydrogen bombs. Hillary, Trump, the Reverend Jesse Jackson, Caitlyn Jenner, Walmart cashiers, Queen Elizabeth, Glenn Beck, Rougned Odor—they all stink.

The comment section of Dr. Nandi's post about thunders down under is hilarious. Posters from Africa and India and all over tell tales of noxious emissions that literally got them removed from conference rooms and vehicles. The stories are eye-wateringly funny.

Married women from every place on the planet proclaim that they will now live eternally thanks to their husbands.

So clearly there are health benefits from cutting the cheese—the average person toots 14 times daily—and Dr. Nandi joins sophisticated folks like Ben Franklin who said "fart proudly" and Louis C.K. who quipped "'you don't have to be smart to laugh at farts, but you'd be stupid not to" in the never-ending quest to make heinie hiccups more socially acceptable.

I once heard a truism at a funeral where a son was eulogizing his father saying his dad insisted: "There's never a time when a fart isn't funny."

And now they are good for you, too! So, if you're near me one day and a silent but deadly event should occur making me giggle just a little—you're welcome.

Mark K. Campbell is the editor of this paper and thinks this sounds cheaper than Obamacare.

# The (Funky) Story Behind the (Stinky) Column

Sometimes here at the paper, we let folks know how we shot a particular picture that we ran. We call it "The Story Behind the Photo."

I thought I'd use the same approach to discuss a column from June 15, "Stink to think: Loving Your Body Emissions."

Of all the columns I've written—this is No. 1,231, one every week since Aug. 13, 1992—I got more feedback on the passing gas column than perhaps any other.

Here's the story behind the column.

When I first stumbled onto the Facebook post that detailed a doctor from Michigan proclaiming that pooting was not only good for the person doing so but for those in the nearby vicinity, it cracked me up.

The doc said gassy emissions could actually make you smarter. *And* those around you!

The comments section of the post—filled with a sizeable group of foreign folks sounding off—was even more hilarious.

But was tooting a suitable topic for a newspaper column?

Also, I've always been leery of the word fart. Because it was verboten to speak in my childhood, it's always been a "dirty word"—that's why there are so many euphemisms for it.

It gave me a chance in the opening disclaimer to use "f-word" when most people think of that *other* f-word.

Nothing will draw a reader in faster than warning them that they might not like or might be offended by what they're about to read.

I considered a long poem; after all, smart and fart rhyme. But I settled on a straight column. The problem became figuring out how to keep bringing up the act of passing gas and making it as palatable as possible.

And I didn't want to write the word fart a million times.

So, I went to the writer's best friend, Google, and typed in "words for fart."

Oh, my.

One site offered 300 different ways to reference the exiting of funky gas from humans.

Many, naturally, were not suitable for publication.

Some sounded better aloud than on the page: "stepped on a duck" for example.

I passed on many other options. "Back draft" would've been funny to firefighters and, while they were referenced in the column, the common man likely didn't know what a true backdraft (a "smoke explosion") was.

I skipped on a slew of other euphemisms like "belch from behind" and "insane in the methane." I also wanted to avoid the word "butt" which knocked out a bunch of them.

Aside from everyday mentions of the act—i.e., let one rip—I settled on four from the website: backside ballistics, thunders down under, heinie hiccups (which I took out then put back in), and my two new favorite words: trouser trumpet.

So, I wrote the column then let it percolate overnight. Upon rereading the next day, if it was too gross or dumb, I'd just kill it.

However, it still made me chuckle—trouser trumpet!—and I decided to go with it, knowing it was unlikely to be a Pulitzer Prize finalist.

I took out one joke and inserted something I thought of while driving in to work, referencing the infamous *Blazing Saddles* campfire scene.

Our proofreaders here also thought the piece was humorous; that's always the main thing to me: Is it funny?

So, "Stink to Think ..." went to the press. Then I waited. Was it too far? Too juvenile? Too gross?

To my relief, almost every person who commented said they liked it. A preacher said he read it to his wife and they loved it. Some Fort Worth firefighters I ran into in a local restaurant said they could relate. And several other folks said they enjoyed the column as well.

Only one lady hated it enough to write a letter to the editor the next week.

If nothing else, at least I now can say trouser trumpet for the rest of my life.

Mark K. Campbell is the editor of this paper and admits that the Bride was not all that amused. Again.

*A reader once told me that every time a column had some play-like dialogue in it, he would read it aloud to his wife in different voices. That made me smile. This column is 100 percent true, and, with seven grandchildren, it's still going on. This was written April 26, 2018.*

# Generational Mind-Numbing Circumstances

It goes like some form of this every time we meet:

BELOVED GRANDCHILD: Hey, Poppy?

ME: Yes?

BG: Can I tell you something?

ME: Yes.

BG: In Breath of the Wild ...

ME: (*eyes glazing over*) OK.

BG: When you're in the other realm, you turn into a wolf.

ME: Uh-huh.

BG: You turn into Link when you leave the Twilight World.

ME: Really?

BG: When you're a wolf, ninjas can ride on your back.

The video game Breath of the Wild is driving me crazy. It's all the kids talk about. Of course, a few months ago, Minecraft was all they talked about. (Thank heavens they haven't gotten to Fortnite yet.)

The only break from Breath of the Wild comes when we're in the car.

BG: Poppy?

ME: Yes?

BG: Can I tell you something?

ME: Yes.

BG: Do you want to play I Spy?

ME: (*eyes glazing over*) OK.

BG: I spy something blue.

ME: My shirt?

BG: No.

ME: Your shorts?

BG: No.

ME: That book?

BG: No.

ME: I give up.

BG: It was that sign we drove past a while ago.

Fortunately, I have experience with this sort of conversation. Thirty-five years ago, the BG's mother did the same thing. Only it wasn't I Spy, and it was before video games. She'd sit in my lap, and we'd watch old *Batman* TV shows.

LITTLE BG MOM: Dad?

ME: Yes?

LBGM: Can I tell you something?

ME: Yes.

LBGM: (*in one breath*) Did you see that part where Batman was tied up? And Robin was also tied up? And the Joker was laughing? And Batman and Robin got away? And they beat up the Joker? And they got in the Batmobile? And they went into the Batcave? And they saw Alfred? And they have Batpoles? And then ...

ME: Yes! I saw all that! I was sitting right here with you!

LBGM: (*unfazed*) Did you see the part where the Batphone was ringing? And the part where ...

ME: Yes! I. Was. Sitting. Right. Here.

Eventually, in a moment of brilliant parenting, I came up with a method to stop the incessant jabbering: "Three sentences!"

She got three sentences to tell me what she wanted me to hear even though I had just seen it. And we counted the sentences out loud. This soon solved the endless run-on did-you-see? questions.

Today, even as adults, if someone in our family goes on too long, you'll hear, "Three sentences!"

I haven't whipped this out on the BGs yet—mainly because first I kinda want to see a ninja ride on a wolf.

Mark K. Campbell is the editor of this paper and is also steeling himself for another round of homemade puppet shows.

*Seeing a couple of guys' gyrations when meeting and greeting each other sent me down the hand jive rabbit hole. I lived through a series of alterations of how humans said hi or celebrated, and, of course, ours in the 1970s was way cooler. I have taught my grandchildren to "give me some skin" followed by "on the "black side" (the back of my hand). It's fun! This was written March 14, 2002.*

# Hand Jive History

It's getting harder to be cool.

The other day I saw a couple of twentysomethings greet one another. The hand jive was quite complex, much more so than in the super groovy '70s.

Way back in ancient days (even before I was born!), men greeted each other with kisses. Then everyone got sick with germs and no one lived to 40. You don't see that greeting among men too often today down at the coffee shop. The simple handshake came into being which relieved many men of the heebie-jeebies of being tickled by another guy's beard.

(I'm leaving out secret handshakes used by college fraternities and those men's groups that meet in double-veiled secrecy and involve sitting in special chairs where the leader wears a Cap'n Crunch hat.)

Naturally, kids don't want to shake hands like their fathers; how uncool would that be? So, hand jive began.

In my teenage years, we "high fived" greetings. That entailed slapping one another's hand held aloft above the head. We also used that technique during athletic competitions; high fives were passed out freely after touchdowns and big baskets. They were simple enough that even white guys could do it.

Later, the arms dropped, and we slapped hands at the waist level, palm to palm. Then you flipped your hand over and said, "On the black side." That wasn't any kind of slur—it was an innocent tribute to our black brothers (who were not "African-Americans" yet).

Even later, we interlocked thumbs for a "soul brother" shake. At the same time, we usually said, "What's happenin', blood?" We called each other "blood" and that was a good thing. Of course, we got it from the black guys. There was a unity in being "blood." I still have to stop myself from "blood"-ing someone when I greet them. It's as ingrained in my vocabulary as "dig" and "happenin'."

The soul brother shake was followed by closed fists that were bumped vertically as if playing one potato, two potato.

In the '80s, handshake greetings morphed even more. Thumb locking soon required other hand gestures like pulling on the ends of fingers then slapping each side of the hand. That's where I got left behind.

The twentysomethings the other day had added the fist knock, knuckle to knuckle, followed by the chest bump. With the latter, greetings are quickly venturing into violent territory. It could get really physical for a guy if you do it during a coed softball game and the catcher's husband is in the stands.

Some sociologist one day will surely see that the handshake has gotten more violent as the world became more chaotic. Studies will be done on football players who assault the guy on their team who just scored the winning touchdown with more violence than from any effort from a foe.

From a kiss to a friendly clasp to bodies crashing together ... what IS happenin', blood?

*Even for the regular array of diets that march past annually, this one was ridiculously strict. It gave me several chances to be snarky and mock celebrities in general. Plus, it has a very queer Madonna joke that was really an eye-rolling s-t-r-e-t-c-h and a half. This was written May 9, 2013.*

# Sticking a Fork into the Latest Dieting Craze

People hate a lot of people and a lot of people hate Gwyneth Paltrow even though *People* magazine named her the most beautiful of all people.

You just can't tell about people.

People despise other people for a variety of reasons, and Paltrow fits almost all of them: born of excess and privilege; lovely and thin even at 40; Academy Award winner; married to a rock star (well, kinda—Chris Martin is the lead singer of Coldplay, the modern-day equivalent of Air Supply); and mother of children with weird names Apple and Moses.

But it's her most recent cookbook—yes, there's more than one—that has so many riled.

Here's a summary of *It's All Good*: Don't eat anything. The end.

Paltrow's food intake suggestions are incredibly restrictive. The list of things she allows is far shorter than the roster of food she disdains.

And, boy, does she disdain.

You have a shot to look like Paltrow if you no longer consume meat. Or soy. Or bread. Or sugar. Or eggs (well, no chicken eggs; Dodo eggs are all right). Or alcohol. Or shellfish. Or potatoes. Or tomatoes. Or wheat. Or corn. Or eggplant (well, I'm okay with that one, actually). Or coffee. Or bell peppers. Or even deep-water fish.

Now, I don't know which fish are deep-water—Kraken, I suspect. I never ask fish where they hail from. If they are fried or blackened, it hardly matters; they will get eaten.

Aside from being generally snooty, Paltrow is sure her way is the right way for humanity to advance as she regularly notes on her website goop.com.

She abhors anything that tastes good, apparently. Paltrow has been quoted with: "I'd rather die than let my kids eat Cup-of-Soup." (Which is apparently popular across the pond; Paltrow has taken up residency in England much more successfully than another high-profile American, Madonna, whose efforts to speak British often sound like a sturgeon [why, yes, that is a long stretch to combine the Material Girl's "Like a Virgin" with a deep-water fish. I apologize].).

According to one person (likely munching on a Ding Dong), if you want to look like Paltrow, you'll have to fork over $300 a day even though almost none of it is for actual food.

According to womenshealthmag.com—which seems a good place to check because most cookbooks are sold to women—there are four types of women's bodies:

1. Pear
2. Straight
3. Curvy
4. Athletic

Following Paltrow's diet could lead to the creation of a fifth body type—Gwyn-orexic, coined by that journalistic bastion, the *New York Post*.

Here are male body types:

1. Dude, you're fat
2. Try lifting a barbell sometimes
3. Slow-pitch     softball     I-can-smoke-and-play-shortstop-at-the-same-time flabby
4. Move-around-in-the-shower-to-get-wet skinny

One of Paltrow's sample meals that is less peasant-like and more semi-normal is mango and avocado salad with balsamic lime vinaigrette.

I assure you that none of the male types are going to eat that; they know that salads get in the way of real food, i.e., steak.

Still, Paltrow has a legion of followers who believe that she knows what she's talking about—after all, she's a celebrity.

But she doesn't sound like a ton of fun at a party. And if she starts singing, well, I suggest releasing the Kraken.

Mark K. Campbell is the editor of this paper, and he would not eat one thing out of that cookbook.

*This is one of the most popular columns I ever wrote, according to readers and some contest judges. Aside from being an award winner, it was another example where I wrote something on one day, wondered if it was too much the next day, then decided to leave it in. This was written July 9, 2009.*

# Hitting the (Sea) Wall With a 2-Year-Old Boy

Some senior citizen recently said he knew the secret to staying fit: just follow a two-year-old boy around and do everything he does.

No truer words have ever been uttered.

The Bride and I just concluded our first-ever vacation-alone-with-grandson—and, boy, was it exhausting.

Dreemi, Poppy, and Link, the first boy in our family in 23 years, settled into a Galveston hotel. The weather was brutal on the coast—apparently, the sea breeze was on vacation, too. Submerging into the lukewarm gulf, flat as a lake, offered little relief. Between the sun and humidity, Galveston made Houston feel like the Rocky Mountains.

Any trip outside resulted in instant sweating, even if you had scored the closest parking space at the hotel. It was no treat inside the hotel, either. Way too many things in hotel rooms are placed at 2-year-old eye level: tissue holder, floor safe, air conditioning controls, and toilet paper dispenser. Link took advantage of all these hands-on activities, especially the latter; the maid must've thought we were in constant gastric distress, judging by the rolls of T.P. we went through. (She also probably wondered why the heat pump was on.)

Link likes to go to sleep watching a movie. It's now possible I have seen *Kung Fu Panda* and *Veggie Tales Lord of the Beans* more than any other human. Even worse on the trip down was the music tape we listened to. A decades-old Disney recording, it was the same cassette our daughters had grown up with. But, thanks to a massive traffic back-up because of just *100 feet* of lane closure in Houston that killed traffic for *five miles*, seven hours of "The Bear Went Over the Mountain" almost did me in.

I don't know who is responsible for "The Bear Went Over the Mountain"—maybe it's some majestic Negro spiritual, perhaps sung by Mahalia Jackson, or the song could be a parable about the grass being greener on the other side—all I know is I hate that bear!

These are the lyrics, sung to the tune of "For He's a Jolly Good Fellow": *The bear went over the mountain/the bear went over the mountain/the bear went over the mountain/to see what he could see. And all that he could see/was the other side of the mountain/the other side of the mountain/the other side of the mountain/was all that he could see.* (The bear also went to the other side of the river with the same results.) Then, for some reason, he becomes a "jolly good fellow!" After 2,000 playings what I wanted to be on the other side of the mountain/river was 1,000 hunters armed with massive jolly good bear traps!

Anyway, Link has mastered the skill of jamming massive amounts of food into his mouth then letting it tumble, half-chewed, out onto the table. (Child rearing experts say to not make a big deal out of this "phase," but the patrons at the IHOP clearly disagreed.)

Link speaks like this: *Gibberishgibberishgibberish* ... **milk**! and *Gibberishgibberishgibberish* ... **truck**! It's amusing.

Night at the hotel was also a chore. Link sleeps like Curly of the Three Stooges when he drops to the floor and goes *woo, boo, boo, boo, boo!* spinning in a circle. Link does the same, rotating in the bed like a human pinwheel, directing kicks at all body parts, many quite delicate, while muttering *Gibberishgibberishgibberish* ... **below the belt!** I considered driving down to Academy for a cup to sleep in.

Later, we wasted money at an aquarium. The one at Moody Gardens is very cool, but, despite sharks, sting rays, and massive schools of fish swimming inches from him, Link couldn't have cared less; all he was interested in was running up and down the ramps. He went ramp crazy! We could've saved a lot of cash by just parking in a handicapped zone.

I managed to get in a couple of runs, and they rank as the most brutal of the thousands of miles I've jogged. In direct sun, no wind, and super humidity, it was God's version of waterboarding. They should send the Guantanamo boys to Galveston—that'd get some answers fast. Afterward I staggered into the hotel, sweat-drenched and red-faced among the guests, jabbering *gibberishgibberishgibberish* ... **water!** as mothers steered frightened children away.

But, aside from R-rated diapers and nocturnal bullseyes jolting me out of dreams of sneaking up armed with a tommy gun on goofy bears crossing mountains, it was a vacation to remember.

*A few times a year, I wrote an entire column as a "playlet." I never shied away from religion because it's a great topic to make jokes about and some people take it stone-cold seriously. Like I wrote in another column in this book, I hope God has a sense of humor or I could be in big trouble. This was written Nov. 18, 2004.*

# A Thanksgiving Piffle, Hold the Blasphemy

I would not be surprised if it went something like this:

ME: Whoa! I'm dead!

THE LORD: YEAH.

ME: It was a bear, wasn't it?

THE LORD: WELL, YOU'RE ALMOST IN HEAVEN SO IT HARDLY MATTERS NOW.

ME: Stupid bears!

THE LORD: IF YOU MUST KNOW, YOU GOT HIT BY A BUS.

ME: Oh ...

THE LORD: RUNNING FROM A BEAR.

ME: I knew it!

THE LORD: FORGET IT! LOOK WHERE YOU'RE AT! REJOICE!

ME: You know, Creator, if I may, some back on Earth think talking in all caps is annoying.

THE LORD: Oh, sorry. Don't want to "annoy" you—especially since it's time to review your life right now.

ME: Oh, dear. Actually, it's not that annoying.

THE LORD: Uh-huh. Speaking of annoying, let's see how you spent the time I granted you to serve Me on Earth.

ME: Yeah, about that ...

136

THE LORD: Don't worry. After all, it's too late to change anything now, isn't it?

ME: Unless this is some kind of *It's a Wonderful Life* thing ...

THE LORD: It's not.

ME: Oh, dear.

THE LORD: Let me just turn this on ...

ME: Why are you using an old movie projector?

THE LORD: I think it looks cooler.

ME: Uh, okay.

THE LORD: (*projector whirring in the background*) Man, you really wore that Earthly body out. Played sports. Hiked. Fished. Lifted weights. Ran over 17,000 miles. Impressive.

ME: I was a big fan of "the body being a temple" thingie, er, verse.

THE LORD: Of course, you can tell me which verse that was.

ME: Uh ...

THE LORD: You know, I gave everyone a book to handle every little thing that could possibly come along in a lifetime. Was it asking too much to read it occasionally? All everyone does is watch TV! What's up with that?

ME: Uh ...

THE LORD: And boy did you watch TV! Look at that—you watched *The Simpsons* a lot.

ME: Yeah.

THE LORD: I mean, a *lot*!

ME: Yeah. Sorry about that.

THE LORD: How many times can you watch a cartoon episode over and over?!

ME: Okay! Sorry!

THE LORD: And you didn't exactly go around spreading the Good News as much as you could've.

137

ME: I always felt a little weird about pushing my views on others.

THE LORD: You really shouldn't—look out! There's a bear behind you!

ME: Aiieee!

THE LORD: Not really! Woo-hoo, it's a hoot knowing what scares everybody! You know, no one has fun anymore. When did my children get so serious about everything? So many people seem to have so little fun. Hmm, that'd make a good bible verse ...

ME: Well, I tried. It seemed like everybody got so easily offended.

THE LORD: Oh, well. Mankind ... what are you gonna do? Oh, my, let's face it: In your life you did a ton of stuff wrong.

ME: I know. I figured there'd be more time to get things right.

THE LORD: That's what they all say. But you did some good stuff, too. You said thanks often; a Father really likes hearing that.

ME: I *was* thankful. For good health, for having a great wife and good kids and a job and a house and ...

THE LORD: I heard you. You're welcome. And it gets better. Because you believed, check this out. (*sweeps with a hand*) Heaven!

ME: WOW!

THE LORD: Now who's talking in all caps?

ME: Are my aunts here?

THE LORD: Yep.

ME: My little brother?

THE LORD: Yep.

ME: Grandmother?

THE LORD: Yes.

ME: Friends and cousins and ...?

THE LORD: Right over there. ,

ME: Yeah! Thanks, Lord!

THE LORD: A wonderful eternity begins now.

ME: If I'd known how cool this was, I would've worked so much harder for You on Earth!

THE LORD: (*sighing*) That's what they all say.

*The story this column is based on seemed more like something you'd find in* Mad Magazine *instead of* Texas Monthly. *It seemed so dumb, yet it was 100 percent sincere. I'm not exactly a cosmetics expert and prove it below. This was written Dec. 10, 2015.*

# Avoid Getting Browbeaten This Christmas

I'm pretty sure I have discovered a Christmas present for women—and maybe a few men—who have everything.

After all, who doesn't want their eyebrows to look better?

Until I married a female, I had no idea how important things like eyebrows and eyelashes were.

1978 BRIDE: Ah, look at those long eyelashes on that sweet baby!

1978 ME: What baby?

It's been my experience that males don't notice or much care about eyebrows or eyelashes—on anybody.

However, it's a really big thing to some. That fact was driven home when I came upon an "advertisement Q&A" in the back of a recent *Texas Monthly*.

The person being interviewed was a beauty-conscious woman ironically named Natalie Plain. Really.

She is the CEO of Billion Dollar Brow. Ms. Plain begins, "When I was young, my mom took me to a brow professional in Beverly Hills."

Now, I don't know about you, but my parents did not take me to Beverly Hills when I was a child. We once went to Lake Texoma and camped out, using defunct electric blankets as ground flooring where you'd wake up the following morning with the control knob jammed into your back.

At Beverly Hills, Ms. Plain said the experience made her feel "special and polished." But things got away from her; later, at college, she confessed that she had "over-plucked" and did not look her best.

Employing her American can-do spirit, she created a moisturizer called Brow Boost then expanded into more products.

In the magazine, she kindly issued a tip for keeping your brows looking their best: "symmetry, symmetry, symmetry."

This is not advice that former Congressman Jim Wright followed, certainly. Ms. Plain must've bolted upright in bed, screaming, whenever she dreamt of the wild-browed public servant.

The Brow Buddy helps you find that elusive symmetry, because—let's face it—you don't want to look like an idiot with one brow flat-lined and the other resembling the Gateway Arch in St. Louis.

Fortunately, many of us around here are eyebrow aware: "Texas fans have been some of the most vocal eyebrow enthusiasts around," said Ms. Plain. I'm pretty sure that sentence had never existed in the history of mankind until that December *Texas Monthly*.

Billion Dollar Brow is on the cutting edge of brow fashion, noting that in some parts of the world, "there is some resistance to the 'modern' eyebrow," Ms. Plain said. Not in Texas! "Texas women are eager to embrace their best brows."

So, if you're struggling for a Christmas gift that shows you are a fashion-friendly person, you might want to consider something from Billion Dollar Brow.

As for me, I'm waiting for Zillion Dollar Nose Hair or Quadrillion Dollar Ear Hair cosmetics because I am the reigning Jim Wright there.

Mark K. Campbell is the editor of this paper and has also been cursed with "thin lips."

*This column had a long life. After receiving good feedback locally—that's a pretty hard title to resist!—I entered it in some awards competitions where it won at each stop. At the national level, it was reprinted in the contest winners' publication. Later, an editor from Minnesota wrote me, saying he liked it and ran it in his paper. All told, this piece was around for about 14 months. This was written May 13, 2004.*

# How Many Cow Brains Could *You* Eat, Tough Guy?

*Warning! The highly informative stuff that follows this paragraph contains graphic words like "vomit" and "diarrhea" because I'm only going to be able to say "retch" and "hurl" and "gastrointestinal freak-out" and "bowels in an uproar" so many times. So, if these sorts of things bother you, you'd best mosey over to the editorial page and read something that almost certainly doesn't involve body functions. Thank you.*

We begin: Did you know there is such a thing as The International Federation of Competitive Eating? The IFOCE says it's "America's fastest growing sport" and judging from how fat most people are today, that sounds about right.

Their official emblem is a guy hunkered over, ralphing into a trash can. Ha! Not really! It's actually too difficult to tell what's on that emblem at www.ifoce.com. It's either lions or horses wrapped in some kind of noodles; but the emblem eating record is 46 in two minutes. Well, I made that up (I think), but there are plenty of other records you can marvel at.

You'd think that competitive eating would be the ideal sport for us fatties. Aside from bowling and golf, of course.

But, as you may know, the world record hot dog eater is a non-fatty, a scrawny 132-pound Japanese guy named Takeru Kobayashi (which translates to "hubcap-sized Mylanta"). He holds the world record of 50.5 hot dogs (with buns) eaten in 15 minutes. He wussed out of last year's championship on Coney Island by eating just 44.5 dogs.

Watching him compete is pretty nauseating: Kobayashi dips the hot dogs in water before downing them. The thought of all that mushy bread—ugh! What's grosser than that?

Well, this: He also holds the record for consuming cow brains. He ate 57 in 15 minutes. (I don't know what he dipped the brains in, probably tequila.) In case you didn't know, 57 cow brains weigh 17.7 pounds.

(We could pontificate here on who originally thought of eating a cow's brain. How hungry would you have to be?! But then we'd have to get to other animal parts records—like the 3.3-pounds of beef tongue a guy ate in 12 minutes. [What does a taste bud taste like?])

Other memorable folks are lauded by the IFOCE.

If you're an older guy looking for an eating hero— for some reason—keep Richard LeFevre in mind. He's 58 years old and just 135 pounds. He once ate 6 pounds of Spam "from the can" in 12 minutes. LeFevre also wolfed down 1.5 gallons of chili in 10 minutes.

The current rage in competitive eating is shorter contests, 8 to 12 minutes. But LeFevre is a "distance man" who excels in 30- to 35-minute events involving "beef and other heavy foods."

Astonishingly, he has a wife; Carlene is— shocking!—also a competitive eater. She created the

"Carlene Pop" which is a bobbing motion that "helps tamp down food" in the stomach.

I'm guessing the LeFevres get few barbecue invites.

You'd think a guy named Cookie Jarvis would hold the Oreo record, but he actually shines in other realms. Checking in at a svelte 409 pounds, he once gulped down 1 gallon, 9 ounces of vanilla ice cream in 12 minutes. But I'm more impressed with his mark of 4 pounds of corned beef and cabbage. Surely there's a fistfight at the plumber's shop when they hear something's stopped up at the Jarvis house.

There's another woman profiled on the website. Sonja Thomas was up for the 2003 IFOCE Rookie of the Year. Despite weighing just 105 pounds, she has ingested 5.5 pounds of deep-fried asparagus in 10 minutes; 157 chicken wings in 32 minutes; 4 pounds, 14.25 ounces of fruitcake; and 65 hard-boiled eggs in 6:40. Amazingly, she remains single.

But what if you dated her?

DENNY'S WAITER: Can I help you?

YOU: Get whatever you want, Sonja.

SONJA: I'd like 65 hard-boiled eggs. And do ya'll have fruitcake?

YOU: Whoa! I'll just have six pounds of Spam.

It's hard to say what the most remarkable record is—18 dozen oysters in 10 minutes? 28 reindeer sausage in 10 minutes (try finding *one* reindeer sausage today)? 33.5 ears of corn in 12 minutes?—but my money is on Donald Lerman.

He ate 6 pounds of baked beans in 1 minute, 48 seconds. Soon after, he set another record: The first time in history a brand-new Port-A-Potty was simply taken straight to the dump.

145

I know a little about big eating. I once ate 17 Dreamcicles in one sitting. But, I'm not ready for international competition.

However, maybe you are. Check out the website for tournaments. But, sorry, you just missed the pickled egg competition. It was held in Texas last month.

Hey, I made it through the whole column without saying vomit or diarrhea. Cool.

*I always consider anything that happened to me fair game for a column. Even this, the stupidest thing I've ever done and one of the most embarrassing. Readers got a kick out of it, they said. It made for some funny reading and, hopefully, someone learned something. I know I did. This was written Jan. 6, 2010.*

# Lessons Learned from 'The Shotgun Incident'

There's just never an instance when a gunshot coming from the back room is good.

(Already, in this first column of 2010, we begin with a warning: DON'T EVER DO THIS! There, that's better.)

When I was a firefighter last decade, we would always examine any major incident, trying to see where we could improve. We called the paperwork (ah, there was always paperwork) "Lessons Learned."

The Bride and I were digging through my mom's place on Lake Whitney. Now that she's moved to Wichita Falls, she needed a few items like her TV, boom box, and electric blanket. And she said I could have dad's old guns.

Now, while I am a macho man in many ways—for example, my current car doesn't have a heater, and it's been a harsh winter—I have never owned a gun. I have, though, seen lots of them used willy-nilly in Mel Gibson *Lethal Weapon* movies, and I got a multi-fire pellet gun for Christmas. So, I knew a little about guns. A little ...

On the gun rack at Mom's place: a BB gun, a pellet gun, and a 12-guage shotgun. Guns are so manly! Naturally, being a multi-generational Texan, I gravitated to the shotgun. I admired its heft and the smoothness of the weapon over by the bed where Mom's electric blanket resided under several layers of comforters and blankets.

I knew that a 12-guage was an impressive gun, and that I could fell all sorts of animals and feed my family if our survival seed crisis garden should fail.

The weapon was so simple. While the Bride gathered CDs in the front room, I pulled back the trigger, and it clicked into place. Then, I tried to get it to go back. (I'm not exactly up to date on gun terminology here—I don't know if "go back" is exactly correct.)

Well, the trigger wouldn't go back. There was only one thing to fiddle with on the gun and the thingie that breaks the gun in half didn't. So, I have the trigger back and can't get the gun to open. Clearly, I have just one option. (Once again, DON'T EVER DO THIS!)

Despite knowing the Lone Star axiom of "an unloaded gun is not a gun," I figured what were the odds of Dad keeping a loaded shotgun in the house? Loosely holding the 12-guage in my right hand, I nonchalantly pointed the barrel at the bed. And pulled the trigger. (I'm not stupid—I aimed it at something soft.)

Yes, it was loaded. And, yes, it was incredibly, shockingly, ear-ringingly deafening. I now do not believe that Mel Gibson can shoot a shotgun one-handed. The recoil was tremendous. The pointy break open thingie— which did work later; I just hadn't pushed it hard enough— kicked back into the webbing between my thumb and forefinger, deep enough that I could see a huge gap where "you idiot!" echoed around inside my hand.

*CSI Lake Whitney* will have a field day gathering up chunks of my flesh formerly attached to me. (You'd be amazed at how often you use the webby part of your right hand: pickle jars, doorknobs, weightlifting, even typing where hittingthespacebarcansometimesbeaproblem.)

The Bride rushed back to the bedroom, and, seeing I was not dead or seriously injured, began laughing. But there *was* carnage. The bed not only got blasted by the gunfire, but the 12-gauge had not been discharged in so long—at least four years—that it's possible that I projected a family of spiders or a dirt dauber's nest into Beautyrest heaven at 750 mph.

The bed was now an ex-bed. The Bride laughed harder and harder as each ravaged layer of the bed was revealed; the blast ripped through the comforters, three blankets, the electric blanket, two sheets, a plywood base, and, maybe, through the floor where an unsuspecting raccoon could now be dead under the house.

The electric blanket was savaged, its wires sticking up every which way like a slaughtered octopus. The new one cost $64.

My ears rung, my hand hurt, and my Bride laughed, but the worst was yet to come.

Now, I could've just covered up the incident, saying I got hurt moving something. But I couldn't let the Bride have something of that magnitude to lord over me; at the next church *Newlywed Game,* it would somehow come out.

So, I trudged next door—to my in-laws—where I fessed up that, without being sure if it was loaded ... I fired a gun ... in a house ... into a bed. I spied the same kind of looks I got 34 years ago when the Bride and I announced that we were going to marry: "Oh, no, Paula Kay. Not this one."

In summary, there are plenty of lessons learned here, the main one being: Don't mess with a gun if you don't know what you're doing.

On the plus side, I already have my limit on electric blankets this year.

*If I had to choose a typical column, it would be one like this. It's stupid, absurdist, and barely edited after being spewed out in about 20 minutes. I found that over-reading/proofing made for changing something that was funny the first three times before the humor sheen wore off from familiarity. I let this one be after penning it. This was written July 27, 2017.*

# What to Do if You Find Yourself Inside a Giant Crab

For my birthday, I got one of those I-would-never-read-in-a-million-years books.

It was an obscure science-fiction novel called *The Nets of Space.*

ASIDE ONE: Back in prior decades, there was no electronic device for reading. Like God intended, we held things in our hands while eating at the dinner table—the backs of mustard jars, Rice-A-Roni boxes, etc. I grew up eating at the table. We all had a book or newspaper or Worcestershire ingredients to consume while we did the same with Mom's fantastic suppers. Yes, eating at the table was frowned on by the Etiquette Police led by snooty Gloria Vanderbilt who was rich enough to have butlers read to her at the solid gold table she ate at. (I'm assuming this, since I've never heard of a poor Vanderbilt.) END OF ASIDE ONE

So, at our dinner table, my reading of choice was often paperbacks. They were mighty cheap, always less than a dollar, and covered every genre. (Mine were either horror or about baseball.)

The cool thing about the paperbacks was that they were always the right size to stick in your back pocket and carry around everywhere, when you might find yourself just sitting around with nothing to do or if you got hungry and needed something to read.

ASIDE TWO: As I got older, I always had three things in my vehicle at all times: my baseball glove and cleats; running shoes; and a paperback. Today, those three items have morphed into my asthma inhaler; Gas-X; and extra underwear. END OF ASIDE TWO

Now, back to *The Nets of Space* …

The novel was printed in 1960 which, you might recall—unless you were a bit *too* into it—those were the dawning days of psychedelia and mind-expanding drugs. And not a whole lot was known about those drugs; that's how the protagonist of the novel ended up in the belly of the queen of a race of giant space crabs.

I will attempt to describe the plot of the book which had two major points making me want to read it:

1. It was short, 128 pages.
2. It was about giant crabs who dipped humans into sauce then ate them.

This is one of those psychological/is-this-really-happening? tales that a normal sci-fi reader would abandon if it was, say, 132 pages long.

In the distant future—1990—mankind has conquered space and is ready to head *way* out there in the universe. The world, at peace now, joined together to build three starships, all fueled by "time-gas."

A guy who washed out of the astronaut program bravely saves his fellow spacemen when there was a time-gas leak to which he was exposed. He goes into a coma where he has visions of seeing the destruction of the first two starships and witnessing crewmembers being eaten by giant crabs (after being dipped in sauce).

Coma-man ends up learning that the crabs are ruled by female crabs, that male crabs are subservient. During subsequent comas, the man hears—while in the stomach of the crab queen!—that the crabs are going to venture all the way to Earth—with nets!—to capture mankind … for food.

The man also coma-mind travels (or does he?) to a miniature race that has some groovy technology. Are these episodes far-out flights of mental fancy? Or are they really happening?

Why, it's the latter! Gargantuan, crab-directed nets *are* coming to Earth so we can become crab food. (It took 110 pages for the nets to show up.)

The man dares to coma-travel one more time—it's tough on the body, as you might imagine—to return to the little people (who think he's a god) for their technology to stop the approaching crab hordes.

Can he do it?!

Well, I'd hate to ruin the ending for you. You'll just have to sit down at supper and find out on your own.

Mark K. Campbell is the editor of this paper and may have just set the world record for writing the word crab the most times in a column.

*I love Halloween and tried to write some sort of spooky story every year it rolled around. Sometimes they were very short fiction I had written, other times a personal scary incident. This true story was told to me by a relative. It was written Oct. 23, 2000.*

# A Haunting Tale

Here's a tale of terror, just in time for Halloween.

Back in the days when you could send your children off into the world without constant supervision, young Dewey, his brother Dale, and a couple of friends headed out to go overnight camping one summer afternoon.

It was about a half-mile walk to the Wichita River, through mesquites and red dirt, mostly. Some people might not have thought too much of this kind of terrain, but, like residents of West Texas love their flat land and those murky swamps are adored by East Texas folk, the boys thought they lived in heaven. Wildlife, camping, fishing, hunting—what more could any boy want?

The trek took them to their favorite spot: a cave perched 10 feet above a small flat that stretched off to a shallow off-shoot of the Wichita. The 11-year olds had been there a hundred times, and this trip seemed no different.

They splashed in the red-tinted water—never more than a couple of feet deep in what they called the "tributary"—hunted critters, and just enjoyed being outdoors. They settled down as dusk approached, eating and building a fire. Then everyone staked out their spot in the cave as the sun dropped.

Through the years, they had heard every kind of noise and seen every animal. Or so they thought. They first noticed something weird just after midnight. It was pitch black as the mesquites rattled and creaked, and the water gently bubbled below. Nothing unusual ... until someone looked about 100 feet up the tributary. There was *something* downstream. Moving. Toward them.

Slowly approaching over the water were six globs of light. Each a little bigger than a dog, the boys would later recall, but very distinct. It wasn't fog—they'd seen that a million times over the water. Somehow, these orbs contained some substance as they floated.

The entities came silently up the tributary and toward the flat. The boys lay frozen in their cave—trapped—as the lights drew methodically closer and closer. No sound accompanied them; they simply floated soundlessly toward the cave. Paralyzed, the boys watched the apparitions reach the flat just below them. The lights were dense, thick, but still luminous. Finally, they moved past in their steady pace, still silent, off the flat and back over the water. Then they were gone.

The trees kept creaking, and the sky seemed even darker. The boys stared into the blackness up the tributary where the things had now disappeared. Shortly, they decided that staying in the cave was not a good idea this night. With the super-speed of the terrified, the boys ran the half mile through scratchy pastures to the safety of their homes. They never spent another night in that cave again.

Doesn't everyone have a spooky occurrence from their past that defies description? I sure do.

I'll never forget that time a bright light settled quietly in an isolated country creek bed in the middle of summer at 3 a.m. What was it? I didn't stick around to find out. Later, home seemed safe—until the ever-present chirping of crickets suddenly stopped.

Then I thought I spied a large, weirdly shaped shadow pass by my window ...

*This is me trying to go full Dave Barry, the great humor columnist. The original plan was to get snarky in a single column about every presidential election. But, scrolling through the internet and writing whatever joke came into my mind, it became clear that it was going to take more than one column. This series still cracks me up—and this was before Trump came along. These were written consecutively Nov. 15, 22, 29, and Dec. 6, 2012.*

# Part I: Our Early Funky Presidential History

Boy, were Republican prognosticators wrong: The sun did rise Nov. 7.

Historically, guys who ran for president were considered by the opposition to be the reason the United States would soon crash and burn.

In 1792, George Washington was one popular fellow, being on money and all. Back then, the runner-up in votes became vice president, so the opposition went after Washington's VP John Adams. The Antifederalists ran George Clinton; however, he did not blow the roof off the sucka so Adams was reelected. (I'm pretty sure that this is the only place you'll get funk references when it comes to presidential elections.)

In 1796, it was a battle of the giants—the Washington Whuppin'—with Adams versus Thomas Jefferson. Adams won 71 to 68 even though one card had it even.

In 1800, things hit the fan. Jefferson and James Madison, whose wife made such yummy treats, would tangle with Aaron Burr who would later play *Perry Mason*.

Burr didn't even want to run because of his busy TV schedule, but Federalists put him in the race anyway. After 35 ballots (!), Jefferson finally won when everybody fell asleep after gorging on all those Dolly Madison cakes.

In 1804, Jefferson got George Clinton on the ticket—the first time the pairing ran. But a confused Clinton thought he'd been elected to Parliament; when he found out that wasn't the case, he uttered the popular phrase of the day—"Funkadelic!"—then decided those were good band names.

In 1808, Clinton decided to go for the top spot, but opposing him was Rufus King whose campaign song "Tell Me Something Good" became a big hit for his Rufus relatives in 1974. (Rufus King, having earlier written the lyrics on the back of the Constitution before passing it over to Ben Franklin, knew he had penned a funk classic, but it took a while to fetch it since the document had already been framed and placed in the gift shop.)

Elections continued with everyone saying everyone else was going to ruin America.

In 1824, the House of Representatives chose the president when there wasn't a clear electoral majority winner because Florida's votes never arrived. The House chose John Quincy Adams—apparently, back then, you couldn't chop down a cherry tree without hitting an Adams; they reproduced like Bushes—and immediately cries of "corrupt bargain" broke out. That resolution, Funk 49, was a big hit at the time and was covered by the James Gang in 1970.

Andrew Jackson, whose only jobs appeared to be selling hickory sticks and running for president, finally won in 1828 and 1832.

In 1836, a new party arose, the Whigs, but they could not unseat Jackson's choice to replace him, Martin

Van Buren. Angry, the upstart party flipped their Whigs. (Yeah, I said it.)

In 1848, Zachary Taylor won despite growing concerns about slavery. Every time someone brought it up, he would put his hand to his ear and say, "What? What?" then change the subject by saying what a weird name his VP had, Millard Fillmore.

I could go on, but I'm out of space. Let's just put on some Brothers Johnson "Strawberry Letter 23" and give it a listen: I think you'll vote that it's one fine tune.

Mark K. Campbell is the editor of this paper and thinks this might be the dumbest column ever.

# Presidential History, Part II: Florida ... Again

When we left our survey last week, Zachary Taylor was making fun of Vice-President Millard Fillmore in 1848. That violation of the Mockery Act of 1847 cost Taylor in 1850 when he ate some bad pickled cucumbers on July 4 and was dead five days later. Fillmore's chuckling at the funeral was considered suspicious as was the fact the he owned a pickled cucumber farm.

He finished the term. In 1852, things were calm thanks to the Compromise of 1850—so peaceful that a party called the Free Soilers (make your own joke here) had a nominee. Many ballots were taken before the winner was Franklin Pierce who, in his inaugural address, said, "Man, no one's more surprised than me."

No historian can tell if Pierce did anything, so James Buchanan won in 1856 by wisely declining Fillmore's gift of pickled cucumbers just before Election Day.

Buchanan got out of the politics business in 1860 when he saw that this slavery thing wasn't going away. At first, Republicans attempted to nominate Salmon P. Chase—a rich, white guy, imagine that—but Abraham Lincoln chopped his way into the thick of things. Because the Democrats were split on slavery and states' rights, Lincoln won. His "No vampires, no peace" rally cry was highly popular.

Lincoln got reelected in 1864 as the Civil War raged. Union victories right before Election Day didn't hurt. This time around, he was a majority victor; in '60, a vampire coalition was highly anti-Lincoln as you might imagine and cost him votes.

Whenever there's a big, honkin' war, popular generals have really good chances at being presidents, and that's what happened with Ulysses S. Grant. He wanted a cannon as a running mate but instead got some guy named Schuyler Colfax who was written in by a bunch of giggling Southerners.

Grant was victorious again the next time around, but, with a new vice-president, Henry Wilson, who won a bet that he could get his name on the ballot.

In 1876, there was a great ballyhoo about "scandal" and "reform"—and this was decades before Bill Clinton. Samuel Tilden was beating Rutherford B. Hayes in electoral votes, 184-165, but four states' ballots were still out: Louisiana, Oregon, South Carolina, and Florida. (Yes, Florida—shocking!) There were 20 electoral votes yet to be counted. The House and Senate split on deciding the winner (shocking!), so they asked some guy on the street and he liked the name Rutherford and chose him. (Actually, a commission decided, 5-4.)

Hayes decided this president stuff was way too much hoo-hah, so he did not run again in 1880. Grant tried to return, this time selecting a sabre as his running mate, but James Garfield won. Then he immediately got assassinated.

That made VP Chester Arthur the president, and he said, "This job is more lethal than being an astronaut" so he did not run for re-election.

In 1884, things got ugly. James G. Blaine was the Republican nominee, and he was so oily that he got knifed right before the election.

Still he almost won when news got out about Grover Cleveland's illegitimate son—this was well before NBA players made the concept popular—but the Soloflex-adverse Cleveland won the day.

In 1888, Americans were a tad concerned that their leader was so fat that they voted for Benjamin Harrison. He was the first president to spend a million dollars—and a lot of that was repairing the White House furniture that Cleveland broke.

Now that the chairs were fixed, Cleveland returned to the top spot in 1892, beating Harrison who had the likability factor of "a Nixon."

In 1896, the economy had tanked so voters rolled Cleveland out of the White House and put in William McKinley. His opponent was silver-tongued William Jennings Bryan whose long orations wowed politicians but put too many regular Joes to sleep; they dosed through Election Day and McKinley won.

Mark K. Campbell is the editor of this paper and this will wrap up next week, he promises.

*Here in Part III is the most obscure joke that perhaps no reader got. The "tarpon" reference concerns the Tarpon Inn in Port Aransas, Texas where a Franklin Roosevelt-signed tarpon scale adorns a wall with 7,000 others. The upscale restaurant at the Tarpon Inn is called Roosevelt's.*

# Presidential History, Part III: Just One Part to Go!

When we left off last week, 1900 had just arrived. Contrary to what experts said, the calendar turning from 1899 to 1900 did not cause adding machines across the world to shut down.

Because they could do it back then, a wily group kept President McKinley but forced Theodore "Drunk Uncle" Roosevelt onto the ticket. After McKinley was assassinated, Roosevelt ended up being a good president unless you were a moose or a bear.

In 1908, Roosevelt threw his considerable bulk behind William Howard Taft who had plenty of bulk of his own. Taft defeated orator William Jennings Bryan, running for the top office for the 115th time. He lost again—and talked about it for two months straight.

In 1912, someone gagged Bryan on the convention floor, and, even with Roosevelt running again, Democrats ended 16 straight years of Republican presidents with the election of Woodrow Wilson.

Keeping America out of the Great War (WW I) got Wilson reelected in 1916. At the Republican convention a Roosevelt ran again. Franklin Roosevelt ended up being the vice president on the Wilson ticket. "You can't swing a dead tarpon around here without hitting a Roosevelt," the verbose Bryan said before the Roosevelts pushed him down a flight of stairs.

In 1920, Socialists tallied almost 1,000,000 votes—and this was decades before Barack Obama's victory. Warren Harding won but died in 1923. So, at the 1924 convention, his vice-president, Calvin Coolidge, was picked as the top guy. Not that he wasn't popular, but several politicians turned down the VP job. Eventually, Charles Dawes drew the short straw.

The Democrats met in Houston in 1928 and selected the first Catholic candidate ever, the thrillingly named Al Smith. His ticket was doomed, however, because his running mate was Joseph Robinson from Arkansas and everyone knows that there's no way a guy from Arkansas could ever become president.

In 1932, Herbert Hoover got re-nominated, but the Great Depression hurt him when voting booths were set up adjacent to soup kitchens. FDR was the Democratic nominee along with Texan John Nance Garner; their "New Deal" pledge was the hope of its day and FDR won easily. They repeated their victory in 1936 mainly because there were still a lot of CCC buildings to construct in state parks across the land.

FDR in 1940—without Garner, who feared Teddy Roosevelt might be savaging his Lone Star cattle while Garner worked in Washington—won a third term by vowing, like his Republican adversary Wendell Wilkie, to keep America out of World War II. Oops.

In 1944, FDR was back this time with Harry S (no period!) Truman as VP. They won easily with the backing of the renegade Punctuation Party.

Truman and Thomas Dewey faced off in '48; both candidates were unpopular, but what are you going to do? On Election Night, Truman went to bed thinking he was going to lose, and Dewey paid big money for a newspaper headline to proclaim it. But a third-party, the States' Rights Democratic Party, collected 38 Southern electoral votes and Truman squeaked out a win. He was surprised—and had to return the presidential silverware that had "somehow" been packed in his suitcase the night before. Dewey canceled all his newspaper subscriptions.

When 1952 came along, Truman left office with the lowest approval rating of all time, 22 percent—a number that would not be challenged again until George W. Bush in 2008 with 25 percent, but that's not adjusted for inflation. The lack of advancement in the Korean War hurt Truman; we would not get *M\*A\*S\*H* until years later.

Americans like generals—General Mills and General Motors, for instance—and who better than Gen. Dwight Eisenhower? He ran against a Democrat who after several ballots, boldly told the indecisive conventioneers "Well, OK, I guess"—Adlai Stevenson.

Eisenhower won even with running mate Richard Nixon already proclaiming to everyone who would listen that "I am not a crook. Really. I swear. I'm not. I just sweat like this. I have a glandular condition!"

Mark K. Campbell is the editor of this paper and swears on a stack of "I Like Ike" buttons that Part IV next week will end this series.

# Hail to the End
# of the Presidential Series!

We left our series last with a sweaty Vice President Richard Nixon.

It would only get worse for him in 1960 when he squared off in televised debates with our prettiest president, John F. Kennedy.

The virile JFK was active and peppy and played football; Nixon looked like a football. JFK won after taking great care to get an acronym-friendly Democratic running mate—LBJ—to help the South understand that it's okay for a Catholic to be president. Sadly, not everyone agreed. JFK got assassinated in Dallas in 1963, and, while there were more Kennedys in America than Smiths, Lyndon Baines Johnson took and kept the reins.

Big and loud and 100 percent Texan, he was an Old School politician who would get whatever votes he needed by doing whatever he needed to do. The Civil Rights Act passed only because LBJ stood on Barry Goldwater's foot with his pointy-toed, "roach-killin'" cowboy boots at a meet-and-greet, relenting only when Goldwater "saw the light." Then they each drank a Pearl.

LBJ was big on the Great Society, but some fellers turned on him when the Vietnam War kept escalating. Finally, he said, "I ain't fixin' to go through another four years of this!" and did not run for reelection.

His VP, Hubert H. Humphrey—HHH, for a while there in the '60's, there was a big run on consonants—faced Nixon; by now, everyone was used to his sweating. Also running was George Wallace who managed to win five Southern states and 46 electoral votes on the KKK ticket. Still, Nixon won pretty easily in 1968.

He repeated in 1972. A gift he received as the victor—a cassette recorder—would come back to haunt him. He turned that thing on all the time, and, amid ear-renting renditions of "Hey Jude," he cussed a lot. A *lot*. And, he also okayed a hotel break-in.

Nixon flew away in a helicopter and was replaced by Gerald Ford. A big man and sorta clumsy if *Saturday Night Live* was any indication, Ford dropped a lot of White House high ball glasses. He was so bland that he almost got overtaken by an actor—Ronald Reagan—at the 1976 convention.

The Nixon taint remained, though, and a Democratic peanut farmer from Georgia, Jimmy Carter, won. Despite the popularity of Billy Beer—named after his hillbilly brother—Carter did not last long. Even drunk people could see he wasn't doing much. Carter gets about as many votes for "best president" as Rafael Palmeiro does for the Baseball Hall of Fame.

Our best acting president followed, Reagan. He was awesome at making speeches and chopping wood. Also riding horses. A conservative Republican, he ruled in a time of peace and prosperity, so when it came time to re-up in 1984, he blasted Democrat Walter (Party Animal) Mondale who garnered few votes even with the first female vice presidential candidate, Geraldine Ferraro.

In 1988, Reagan was 119 years old and could not run again. George H.W. Bush, Reagan's VP, did and beat out Pat Robertson's "invisible army"—which he still sees with great regularity today as loved ones pat his hand—to win the nomination.

In 1992, recanting on his "no new taxes" pledge hurt Bush especially when Bill Clinton ran on a "new taxes for everybody!" platform. Folks loved Clinton, and he loved a lot—a *lot*—of them back. He was our most popular horndog president since JFK.

After two terms, the country was no longer dazzled by whatever it was Clinton had, so they elected George W., the other Bush, who has never been called dazzling. It took a special counting of Florida votes and a court verdict, but

Bush eventually served twice, prompting Americans all over to wonder, "What just happened?!"

The media dubbed him the worst president ever. He was given a test to prove otherwise, but he lost it.

We are currently in the second term of Barack Obama who smoked Mitt Romney in 2012. (Well, not literally, even though Obama does smoke.) He's African-American, but what percentage is unknown because he won't produce any sort of paperwork about his past, ever. So far, everything has been someone else's fault. In that regard, Obama is not only the first black president but also the first teenage-acting president.

Mark K. Campbell was elected class Reporter during his senior year in high school.

*Like so many others, this one's pretty silly, but back then, every other commercial was for either, uh, a way for men to recall younger, more vivacious days or for sleep aids. When word got out that after taking Ambien seeking a good night's rest, people were sleepwalking and unknowingly eating, the topic proved too yummy a subject to pass up (sorry). This was written April 7, 2006.*

# What Goes On While You're Taking Your Ambien

Like most humans, I don't sleep well.

It could be a combination of things—concerns about the immigration problem combined with lifting weights at 10 p.m. after drinking four Cokes.

I also apparently have superhuman powers while sleeping. (Of all the superpowers to possess, I get "hearing while asleep.") I am constantly being awaken by the teeniest of noises, like two June bugs duking it out on the kitchen floor.

And, my bladder is now the dominant organ in my body.

Usually, a person does just the wrong things to prepare for bedtime. You shouldn't get in bed except to sleep, experts say. Drinking wine—even bottles that come with corks!—won't help. You should not watch TV in bed.

Well-rested experts say you DO need "white noise" which is not, as you might expect, conservative talk shows yammering on about the upcoming immigration march, but, of course, "noise produced by a stimulus containing all audible frequencies of vibrations" which is dictionary.com's version of "listening to your wife tell you about her day."

Today, however, it's safe to say that the billions of dollars you and I have forked over for important prescription drugs like Levitra and their exceedingly creepy TV commercials have paid off. A new generation of sleep Rx has arisen.

Like Ambien. Naturally, there are some side effects. The televised sleep aid ads, like every other medication commercial, list all possible problems with their drug. Usually that includes "pregnant women should not even *touch* this medication" and "to be safe, keep the drug in the mower shed out back."

In Ambien's case, one drawback—aside from never being able to look directly at the pill—is "somnambulism." That's sleepwalking. Some Ambienians have found "primitive desires" are unlocked in their somnambulistic state. Generally, no one wants that.

For most folks, sleepwalking manifests itself in eating. These primitive desires occur between the deep dream, REM sleep (where you might see shiny, happy people) and the near-waking stage ("man, I should go to the bathroom").

But, if you're really in a bad way, you'll overlook such minor possible setbacks and gulp down a pill. I finally relented and took an Ambien, taking great care to 1) use gloves and, 2) make sure I hadn't accidently grabbed a Levitra.

The Bride took full advantage of my sleepwalking.

First, she duct taped the vacuum cleaner to my hand while holding an Oreo cookie just out of my dazed reach. Unknowingly, I cleaned the entire house.

I also dug out my old electric football game and performed something akin to a superhuman feat: I completed a pass with that dinky piece of "football" cotton!

My player immediately vibrated the wrong direction for a safety, but that hardly mattered. I had performed a miracle!

Next, I apparently sang the entire soundtrack to *The Rocky Horror Picture Show*, acting out all the parts, even Susan Sarandon's "Touch-A, Touch-A, Touch Me" wearing the appropriate feminine attire.

Naturally, all this activity would make anyone hungry, so I trudged to the kitchen. First, I ate the battling June bugs—that shut them up!—then I began feasting on half gallons of Blue Bell, boxes of Fiddle Faddle, that old stash of Christmas fudge, and some Kool-Aid right out of the package. The Bride tried to put some asparagus in my hand, but even in an altered state, I wasn't about to eat that.

After a series of "picking cotton" (an old football warmup exercise that we'd never refer to by that name today), I found my way back to bed and slept.

In an REM frenzy, I dreamt that we had sealed our Texas border by building a giant fence along the Rio Grande then made our state better by putting all the talk show hosts on the other side.

The next morning, I woke up sweaty in a bra with pieces of popcorn stuck around my cherry Kool-Aid-stained mouth. But I was well rested!

So, for those like me who don't sleep well, it's a trade-off. You *will* get some rest on these new drugs. However, your wife will get some killer videos of you.

In any event, at least the house will be cleaner.

*Gas was crazy expensive in 2008, so many people decided to vacation close to home. I figured that meant possibly seeing some wild animals in zoos, wildlife sanctuaries, etc., so I came up with ways to try to survive some animals they might run into. Also: In the headline, I got to reference the Go-Go's and one of their hits, "Vacation." This was written June 26, 2008.*

# Go? Go? 'Staycation': All You Ever Wanted?

The word that will be remembered from 2008 is most likely "staycation." (Well, that and "%$@~&" thanks to gas prices.) With travel and lodging costs so great now, many families are electing to vacation locally, hence "staycation."

Understanding this, it's possible that folks will be visiting zoos, nature centers, and local wild areas. So, as a public service you'll never get from the Big City newspaper, here's a comprehensive list of how to survive animal attacks.

Naturally, the most important facet in avoiding being mauled by critters is to be faster than whomever you are in nature with. But, if you feel guilty about out-running your 10-year-old daughter to the car while a bear bears down on ya'll, you need to read these precautions on surviving animal attacks.

### Alligators

Certainly, there are gators in Eagle Mountain Lake. They are masters of disguise, often donning alligator hats and shoes and sometimes a nice purse to camouflage

THE SNAKE IN THE DISHWASHER

themselves. Then, when you try to get away, all of those accoutrements come off, and there's the real gator.

ESCAPE! The best way to escape an alligator that doesn't yet have your femur in its mouth is to run. While gators are very fast, you most likely will be horrified, and that's a very good state to make some good time with. If you *are* femur-impaired, fight back by gouging three vital gator areas: eyes, nostrils/ears, and the palatal valve. Naturally, you will have to try to remember what the palatal valve is and by then it will certainly be too late. However, the valve—a flap in the gator's mouth that keeps water out—might just be close enough to your patella that you can try to wedge your kneecap in there. Don't count on it, though.

### Monkeys

These critters are almost as tricky as bears—they look cuddly until they have ripped off one of your appendages. The fewer appendages you have, the less likely you are to escape. Monkeys don't just fling poop; they can scratch and bite, and, with their poor hygiene and lackluster dental habits, this can be very troublesome. Don't mock a monkey—the payback is awful and usually smelly. Never show a monkey your teeth, that means a challenge. (This could be the only instance when being a meth addict could actually be beneficial.)

ESCAPE! Since an attack will most likely happen following a zoo jailbreak, try offering the marauding monkey a $4 Coke or a nearby dik-dik. Don't fight back— which will be hard to do when you start thinking that an animal that slings poop is digging its paws into your flesh.

### Killer bees

It takes a lot of training to become a "killer" bee. The top-of-the-bee-chain insects take their rating seriously and will sting the crud out of you. You might be ambling along on your staycation when, oops, thousands of killer bees suddenly descend on you. A natural inclination is to jump into a body of water, but the well-trained bees will just wait you out and then you'll get a lungful of stingers once you surface. Don't swat at bees or flail your arms—according to a government report—because bees are attracted to movement. You should be able to tolerate 10 stings per pound of body weight. While I personally wouldn't kill time trying to do the math while running from an attack, an average adult should be able to handle at least 1,100 stings.

ESCAPE! Run away! Run like a Baptist preacher's coming to the front door! Run like there's a sale at Penney's! Run, man, run! Race for any shelter—car, barn, Neiman Marcus. The best part of the report: "Do not stop to help others." You can make that announcement at your pal's eulogy: "Hey, I wanted to stop to help, but that government report said ..."

### Bears

No animal is eviler and bears are way smart—many can even ride a unicycle! Since they are great climbers, swimmers, and runners, one's choices for surviving are limited. Making noise might keep some bears at bay. Some folks sing, some chant things like "Bear, please don't eat me!" while others wear bells that are often found in ursine scat.

ESCAPE! Do not run, swim, climb, or try to flee on a unicycle—bears are better at all those things than you. Make yourself look bigger by raising your arms; it's better if at the end of one of those arms you have a big ol' gun. You can try some bear spray which will either work or really anger the bear. If it gets to you, curl into a fetal position and play dead. However, if the bear keeps biting you, you might as well try to fight back. Good luck with that.

*Here's a case where I conjured up some ideas on my own then fleshed it out with internet searching. I tried to get a set of women from an array of professions/historical significance. This $10 conjecturing was a hot topic at the time—well, for a couple of days anyway before something else came along to fire up social media. This was written June 25, 2015.*

# Placing the Odds on the First Woman on the $10 Bill

I like women. I married one and reproduced two.

They are remarkable females, but they probably aren't the sort who will end up on the $10 bill in 2020.

A federal law says that living folks cannot be put on U.S. currency.

Likely, that edict will be dashed by 2020, so every possible American woman ever could be up for the honor. It's a tough call.

In today's pop culture society, if an internet poll is taken, whichever booty-shakin' musician who happens to be hot in '20 would get the nod.

But this is a unique honor and requires deep and detailed thought.

So, here's how I see the odds of the first woman to appear on the $10 bill.

**Taylor Swift: 1,000,000 to 1**

In five years, she could be the most famous person on the planet—even though I don't know one of her songs.

**Marilyn Monroe—750,000 to 1**

She would make hipsters and movie buffs happy. By 2020, the bill could contain a 3-D image of her skirt blowing up like in *Some Like it Hot*.

### Caitlyn Jenner—749,000 to 1

The world keeps getting weirder; what better way to pacify the wild-eyed liberal left than putting the former Olympian decathlon champion on the bill?

### Emily Dickinson—600,000 to 1

I love the idea of poetry on a $10 bill. Every time they reissue it, new verses could be put on the bill. I think "because I could not stop for Death/He kindly stopped for me" would make great retirement incentive. Maybe someone would save that $10 and not buy a Coke which will probably cost that much in 2020.

### Amelia Earhart—300,000 to 1

She broke plenty of records but getting lost forever puts a dent in her resume.

### Sandra Day O'Connor—200,000 to 1

The first woman Supreme Court judge should merit consideration, but Democrats will rule against it.

### Sally Ride—100,000 to 1

Back when we were enamored with space travel as a country, the odds for the first female astronaut would've been much better. But too few care in these times.

### Michelle Obama—50,000 to 1

The last eight years have proved that anything can happen.

### Hillary Clinton—50,000 to 1

She's a Clinton, so don't rule anything out.

### Shirley Chisholm—25,000 to 1

She was the first elected black woman to serve in Congress and also vied to be the Democratic presidential nominee in 1972. Her face on a ten would revive her legacy.

### Rosa Parks—10,000 to 1

She got all the press for being a civil rights activist even though others protested before her. Still, she's got the name recognition.

### Harriet Tubman—5,000 to 1

Anyone who was key in creating the Underground Railroad should receive substantial consideration, but I think she'll get cancelled out by ...

### Harriet Beecher Stowe—5,000 to 1

Too many Harriets causes confusion. However, the idea of an author is cool—she wrote *Uncle Tom's Cabin*—and the novel's impact led to changing the nation's views on slavery and blacks.

### Helen Keller—100 to 1

This would be a great choice. Who else overcame seemingly impossible odds—man or woman—to achieve such astonishing success?

### Eleanor Roosevelt—10 to 1

If not for No. 1 below, she makes the most sense; Ms. Roosevelt fought for all races, colors, creeds, and sexual persuasions.

### Oprah—2 to 1

She already owns most of the tens anyway, so we might as well just put her face on them.

Mark K. Campbell is editor of this paper and avoided the urge to nominate his favorite female, Mrs. Baird's.

*My little brother was sick at the same time I was; it was stomach cancer that would kill him in 1997. I feared I had the same—especially since my nausea just would not ebb. It was the first time I'd ever been so ill, and no medical professional could ever pinpoint a specific culprit. This was written May 27, 2015.*

# Can a Song Save Your Life?

On David Letterman's last show, he exited his lengthy TV career to a song by the Foo Fighters, "Everlong."

He mentioned how special the song was to him as he recovered from heart surgery.

I know what he's talking about.

Sometimes, a song takes on some kind of special power, one that affects only you in an indescribable way. And you latch onto it for dear life.

For most of us, "Everlong" is just another rock song. But not for Letterman.

That's how I feel about an obscure song you've probably never heard of, R.E.M.'s "Endgame."

In February 1997—early on the morning of the 27th, to be exact—I, a firefighter, was heading to what would become a 5-alarm apartment fire in Arlington.

But I never made it. En route, I felt left arm numbness, unbelievable nausea, and I started sweating madly.

Holy cow! Was I having a heart attack at 39 years old?!

I spent the rest of the shift in the ER; then, after blood work was deemed okay, I was sent home.

But the symptoms returned, and I began an insane amount of testing to try and figure out what was wrong.

175

I was ridiculously fit then; I rated in the one percentile of humanity on the treadmill stress test. (Oh, to be in such good shape today!)

All test results kept coming back fine. They finally settled on reflux as the culprit, but I knew it was not just that. (A truism: No one will ever know your body better than you.)

So, while I went through proddings and pokings, I would come home—still incredibly nauseated with plenty of anxiety—and plop down in front of our home computer (a behemoth tower in those days).

The machine could play music, and I put in R.E.M.'s *Out of Time* CD then clicked over to "Endgame."

There are no words in the song—just some "da-das." I don't know why I found such solace in the music, but I did.

Somehow, I knew I wouldn't die if that song was playing. Sounds dumb, of course, but I sat there and listened to "Endgame" (appreciating the irony of the title) over and over and over. Day after day. Over and over.

I finally self-diagnosed myself with physical exhaustion. I began taking a few more vacation days. And, weeks later, I started a steady recovery.

Can a song save your life? I don't have solid proof, but I say yes.

Mark K. Campbell is the editor of this paper, and he figured a religious song should've fixed things, but that wasn't the case in 1997 despite plenty of cueing up of DC Talk's "Jesus Freak."

*More than once, I wrote about race relations. I really thought we had a lot of that worked out decades ago. But it kept popping up—along with new words like "transracial" and a slew of other "trans"-prefixed words. When a nationally prominent woman claiming to be black proved not to be, it seemed a good time to remind everyone that, good grief!, we're all the same—human. And the tag at the end of the column is a true story from when I was a firefighter. This was written June 7, 2015.*

# Confessions of a Transracial White Dude

I ain't black.

You know, we thought we had most of this racial business figured out by the mid-1970's.

But somewhere along the decades, things appear to have regressed.

Now, while I'm not black—I'm old enough that African-American seems strange to say, to me and my black friends who are around my age—I'm a lot of other stuff. Everyone is. And, apparently, some folks are "transracial"; they choose what race they are.

It looks like anyone can claim to be any race—at least judging from the most recent news report about a white woman, Rachel Dolezal, posing as an African-American and serving then resigning as the Spokane, Washington NAACP president.

Her parents—from Montana (motto: "Could we BE any whiter?")—have come out and said that, uh, no, Dolezal is not black. A photo from her childhood seems to prove that the smiling blond—resembling a carb-eating Gwyneth

Paltrow—is Czech, Swedish, and German. Good luck getting any whiter than that.

What does all this transracialness mean?

Filmmaker Spike Lee has gone on record as saying that anyone with a single drop of black blood in them is black. Back in the '70's, we never thought 40 years later, all these tags would still be applied—or new ones created.

One of my daughters married a Latino guy. Our granddaughters are as brown as they could be. Like that matters.

Our favorite story from granddaughter Alicia is that, one day in summer after playing outside often as a four year old, she announced, "I'm so brown, I'm almost a full-blown Mexican!"

This really cracked up her mom, my whitest-person-on-Earth daughter.

There are times when, thankfully, race doesn't matter. Sports is great for that; you're a team.

It didn't matter on 9/11.

And we didn't think about race at my previous profession, firefighting. Do you think I cared about what race the guy/gal was who I might need to pull me out of a burning, collapsed building?

Like I said: I ain't black—I'm just an old white guy doing his best, trying to get this racial stuff worked out ... like most other folks. We're transgetalong.

Mark K. Campbell is the editor of this paper and once helped with the delivery of a black baby (which was just like a white baby delivery). It was transgroovy!

*Sometimes coming up with a column idea is easy, and sometimes it's not. It was the latter this week. Sitting at the desk on publication day, I came upon a story about how hippos kill far more people then you'd think. That led to investigating which critters were most deadly and a chance to riff off the list—and the paranoia some folks have about certain creatures. This was written March 30, 2016.*

# Why You Shouldn't Be Eyeballin' a Hippopotamus

Lots of things can kill you—and some might be in your backyard right now! Here's a list of critters that end lifespans of humans, listed by number of people the murderers take out annually.

SHARKS – 10

You'd think sharks would be higher, but they really just have a bad reputation. There are tales about kind bears (Gentle Ben, Smokey), but, as far as I know, there's never been a story about a shark helping people, like leading stranded boaters to land or scooping up exhausted swimmers and letting them ride on their backs to the nearest cruise ship.

ELEPHANTS – 100

These deaths usually come from one of those elephants that plays soccer; they are notoriously poor losers.

LIONS – 100. While the world bemoaned an American dentist killing a lion in Africa last year—who can forget Jimmy Kimmel's crocodile tears on his show—now the felines are so prevalent since the ban on hunting them that sparse African taxpayer dollars are being spent to thin the ravenous herds via gun-toting government officials. Plus, there's the area's loss of tourism. It's lose-lose for the people there—minus the 100 eaten every year, of course—and win-win for the growing population of lions.

HIPPOPOTAMUSES – 500

They don't look like they'd take you out, but these beasts will flat-out kill you if you mess with their staked-out body of water. Or call them fat.

CROCODILES – 1,000

Once again, stay away from the water. However, crocs can make some serious time over land, too. And, even if by some miracle you escape their jaws, you'll likely succumb to some icky bacteria that vacations in their grotesque teeth, leftovers from slower runners.

TAPEWORMS – 2,000

Nobody wants a tapeworm. I don't know what the grossest word in the English language is but tapeworm surely got some votes.

ASCARIS ROUNDWORMS – 2,500

Okay, roundworm isn't much better, just a smidgen higher than tapeworm. In fact, having any kind of worm is bad—even earworms if you get "We Built This City" stuck in your noggin.

FRESHWATER SNAILS – 10,000

If you can't run away from a snail, you probably deserve to die, like if you can't escape from a mummy. But these snails are the kind people actually eat—I assume on a drunken bet.

ASSASSIN BUGS – 10,000

If you have the word assassin in your name, you are surely up to no good.

TSETSE FLIES – 10,000

I have no idea what this bug is, but I've giggled about its name for almost six decades now.

DOGS – 25,000

Remember all those times your dog licked you in your face while you try not to recall where it was licking about eight seconds earlier? Well, one day one of those licks will be paired with teeth. (Cats would probably be in this spot since a recent report said that, if they were bigger, cats would immediately kill their owners. That's why they are evil. [The cats, I mean—well, and some owners.])

SNAKES – 50,000

Most folks die by heart attack after lifting up a rock and seeing one.

HUMANS – 475,000

Let's face it: We're our own worst enemy. Not everyone can resist the temptation to kill the guy who wrote "We Built This City." Still, mankind is mostly good—I said *mostly*.

MOSQUITOES – 725,000

These guys are everywhere, including your backyard. Is one infected with some horrible disease that will take you out buzzing behind you right now? I'm not willing to take that chance; there has never been a good mosquito—I kill 'em all, personally trying to balloon their death rate to rival their human death numbers.

Mark K. Campbell is the editor of this paper and remains more concerned about bears than anything.

*I seem to have written about ducks a few more times than you'd think. Our personal duck, Scott, went from being too cute to too gross, constantly ejecting poop—everywhere, all the time. We finally scooped him up and took him to a city park where we saw through the years that he was happy to poop there, too. If you know the title is a reference to an obscure spaghetti western, good on you. This was written March 19, 2009.*

# Duck, You Sucka!

If I serve no other purpose on this good Earth, let me warn mankind to never buy a duck.

Through the years, I always thought the scourge of the planet was meatloaf. As I got older, it changed to algebra. Then it was screaming parents at pee wee games.

But now I know it's ducks.

I'm not an anti-animal person. I brake for non-venomous snakes and carefully avoid upsetting the elaborate webs of hand-sized spiders. I currently own a dog whose fur is the repository for every speck of beggar lice on our property and who cost as much as a small house thanks to successful surgeries. We also have barn cats which keep us rat-free, but, let's face it, are virtually useless otherwise. Cats are cute when little but can't do cool pet things like catching thrown Frisbees or go swimming with you.

Our duck can be blamed on our youngest daughter who got talked into buying one at First Monday in Weatherford by a hillbilly who danced the Sold Another One Jig as she walked away.

Like cats—and all small animals, except maybe baby snakes which are never very cuddly—ducks are cute when newborn, small puffs of down.

They grow faster than the creature in *Alien*—and are much, much grosser. I'd take 100 slime-dripping aliens rather than ever owning another duck.

The problem with ducks is that they have some kind of bowel problem. Constantly. And they lack the social skills to scoot around to the side of the house. They are the hippies of the animal kingdom, living by a defiant "Do your own thing, baby!"—usually right on the driveway.

Now, I own a water hose and often take the necessary action to remove the problem; however, it isn't that simple since its concrete-staining ability is unrivaled by any other known creature. A duck should be called a "land octopus." Like its tentacled brother, the duck emits a fluid funk that repels invaders. But it ain't ink. (Hmm, what would that sound like underwater?)

Our duck, Scott, is also remarkably amorous, with an eye especially toward one cat. We have no desire at our house to become the *Ranch of Dr. Moreau*—breeders of some sort of unholy merger of animals.

Scott's smart, too. He shamelessly kowtows to the ruler of the property, Sampson, a Great Pyrenees. It's embarrassing and so obvious! How can the other animals not see it?! Scott will preen and clean Sampson, nipping gently at his fur—they even sleep together!—then spy the cat and waddle her way, pooping all the time like that will impress or something: "Hey, you're looking good today." *FSSSSSSSST!* At this point, if ducks could giggle, Scott would.

When he first arrived, Scott had some value. He ate a lot of grasshoppers. Maybe that messed up his digestive tract. But now, he's clearly intent on taking over the property; I don't trust him. Why won't he just fly away? Don't such birds head south?

He'd better head out soon—Thanksgiving isn't that far away.

*Reading* The Lord of the Rings *with its poetry combined with the regularity we'd received poems from readers—and the fact that I made fun of poetry often—I decided to pen a parody based on a true tale I read about a young girl who could not tolerate sunlight. (Hmm, that sounds mean now.) It was supposed to be tongue-in-cheek and fake ultra-serious, but I felt a little bad when a sweet older lady came into the office and asked if the story was real. This was written May 7, 1998.*

# One Little Girl

The bright triangle slid across the floor
and disappeared by nine.
The wall absorbed it by the door
just beyond the blind.
They must have sat her down one day,
she couldn't remember when.
To tell her in a simple way
that she would not see ten.

But she soon found out about the light:
It could not touch her skin.
So, she became a child of night.
"That's how it's always been."
They lived on a lake or rather the slough
back where the creek came in.
Few triangles there on the water blue,
so deep into the fen.

Her parents fretted her sun aversion
Her ventures out were slight.
Could they give her peace or fun
already in her twilight?

184

Early one morning before sunrise
she stepped into the boat.
And crept into undarkening skies
a rare thing in her throat.

Hope! A small boat with a trolling motor
Gave her this unknown thrill,
Let her move on the calm, dark water
Like anyone else, so genteel.
Her parents stood silently on the shore
Not seeing, but they could hear.
Still all the while they both peered for
Feared triangles to appear.

At dawn and dusk she'd cruise the water
Saw many a wondrous thing;
Over there paddled her pet—an otter
"Not a nutria!" she'd sing.
A snake swam by and rubbed her craft
As a cat would a leg.
With splashing turtles she shared a laugh
And gulls zipped by to beg.

Secret deer, a spotted wildcat
Stark still with shiny flanks
And spawning fish with eggs so fat
Splashed the nearby banks.
This was her life for quite a while
And she seemed content.
Coming back at dawn she'd have a smile
Always glad she went.

But despite avoidance of the light
And each precaution filled,

185

Time, as always, won the fight
The tiny boat was stilled.
The bright triangle slid across the floor
It does so every day.
And, as it moved beyond the door,
They put the boat away.

*Embedding book, movie, or song titles in columns is something I did sometimes. The most tune-laden one was a Beatles piece, but this one is funnier. Selling plots on the moon and David "Ziggy Stardust" Bowie made for a perfect match. This was written March 28, 2013.*

# Lunacy? Plots for Sale on the Sea of Tranquility

David Bowie, well-known extra-terrestrial, sang about "The Man Who Sold the World." But Dennis Hope has achieved fame by selling the moon—and you can buy a chunk of it.

He says people are taking him up on this space oddity.

In the 1990s, Hope took advantage of a loophole in the 1967 United Nations Outer Space Treaty that said no country could own the moon—but it noted nothing about *individuals*, so Hope laid claim to the orb.

And now he's selling plots on it.

He's made a fortune hawking one-acre lots for $19.95. (With a "lunar tax" and shipping and handling, the total is $36.60.)

Multiple acres can be purchased at a discounted rate. Someone plopped down $250,000 for 2.66-million acres. (But might it be buyer beware? What if the acreage is on the far side of the moon? Or filled with scary monsters and super creeps?)

And, before you scoff too much, some famous folks—some young Americans, some in their golden years—have already bought moon property. Like former presidents Ronald Reagan, George H.W. Bush, and Jimmy Carter (who's anxious to create a splinter group for Habitat for Humanity—Abodes for Aliens) who all bought in.

If the moon is just too close for you, Hope also owns Jupiter, Mercury, Venus, Mars, and Pluto; he'll let that latter one go in its entirety for just $250,000. (Once a sphere loses planetary status, it's pretty much dead meat; plus, it's so far away—location, location, location.)

Hope is way ahead of the curve on this venture in many ways, always making changes.

For instance, he has created a special monetary system—Deltas—which can be traded for Earth money. Humans can make deposits in the moon's bank here on our planet—then make withdrawals—from Earthly ATMs.

When China was considering building a moon base, Hope warned them to back off, that he'd not flinch at suing them: "Let's dance!"

And, when another guy said he owned the sun and was going to charge Hope for the free energy he was "stealing," Hope told the guy to just turn off the power source—he didn't want the sun's energy. So far, the other guy has not doused the sun.

Big money could await current moon property investors—or their future generations—since Hope projects that under the lunar surface lies $6 quadrillion in helium-3 reserves. Used in nuclear fission, helium-3 currently goes for $125,000 per ounce.

Hope was also sharp enough to set aside parts of the moon as "reserves." Places like the site where U.S. astronauts landed. And the polar regions where Hope said he turned down a $50 million offer to buy the moon's north pole since there might be water there. And with water on the Red Planet, maybe life on Mars? More potential customers.

Hope wasn't the first to try selling off the moon. In fact, he is under pressure and has some serious competition via the Luna Society International which claims to be the *real* owners of the moon. "Earth's Leading Lunar Estate Agency" is letting "the beautiful southern shore" of the Sea of Tranquility go for just $37.50 per acre.

The apparently crappy Sea of Vapors can be snapped up for just $18.95 an acre, but you just know it will soon be covered in spaceships up on blocks and about 100 uncaged, yapping alien dogs.

Mark K. Campbell is the editor of this paper and embedded nine David Bowie songs in this column to hunt for. Happy Easter! Here they are: *Fame; Space Oddity; Scary Monsters and Super Creeps; Young Americans; Golden Years; Changes; Let's Dance; Life on Mars?; Under Pressure.*

*I was a bit worried about this column because every one of our friends has a bigger abode than us, and I didn't want them to think it was about them—even though it kinda was. A few days after its publication, I was going to pick up my eyeglasses in a nearby town when a lady leaving the business stopped me. She asked if I was Mark Campbell (I usually answer that with a cautious "maybe ..."); this time I said I was. She quickly said she loved this column, that she lived in the smallest house in their snazzy neighborhood, and that always bummed her husband. She said she read it to him then clipped it out—and put it into their family Bible. That was pretty cool, I thought. This was written April 12, 2018.*

# The Difference Between a House and a Home

Some of my friends—most, actually—live in large abodes. They are sprawling places with several bathrooms, numerous bedrooms, three-car garages, and man caves.

That ain't the Bride and me.

Our friends are all great people who worked hard to purchase the houses of their dreams. God bless 'em. Those massive structures are impressive with soaring ceilings, elaborate floors, and Italian marble all over the place—including bathrooms.

If there's one thing I envy my friends' expansive houses for, it's a big bathroom. I've lived almost 62 years and never had one of those showers you could punt a football in or been able to towel off without knocking the shaving cream off.

My friends love their houses. But there seems to be something missing in many of them: Their places are curiously vacant. Oh, they are jam-packed with awesome furniture, the biggest TVs, and fabulous accoutrements.

But they still feel stark, soulless, sometimes; they're not empty, but there is a vague dullness, an aura everywhere that oozes sadness, somehow.

That's not every massive house, of course. And, don't get me wrong: I would not sneeze at a bigger place. Our home—lovingly called Crackerbox Palace after the George Harrison song—is hilariously small by today's standards.

Built in 1978, we bought it in 1994. It has three bedrooms, but they're so small that they'd be a sewing or scrapbooking room for today's houses. The washer and dryer are in the garage.

I had house envy for years until I got a life lesson that a house is not necessarily a home.

Because we have relatives south and north of our Parker County home, we were always the central location for everyone to converge in at Christmastime.

And that's what happened for years. From Wichita Falls down to near Waco, family annually drove to the Crackerbox Palace for holiday cheer.

As time wore on, it began to get crowded as families expanded. I figured it was time to start taking the party somewhere else where there was more space.

After all, we were jammed in the Palace now, having to squeeze around while opening gifts and playing games. Wouldn't it be great for everyone to assemble where there was more room?

So, I was more than surprised that everyone said no—they wanted to keep coming to the Palace. We had created memories there, they said; it was festive and fun and being all crammed together was part of it.

Even that time a winter storm arrived. Or when the well pump went out, and we had no water—or tiny bathroom facilities—for 30 people.

"We like coming to your home," they said. "We like how it feels there."

So, the Bride and I don't have the kind of abode you'll ever see on a magazine cover. But feel free to read the publication in our dinky living room.

Mark K. Campbell is the editor of this paper, and the Crackerbox Palace has a phenomenal storm cellar, built into the side of a hill.

*I was so glad to find a format to write this piece of history almost three decades after it occurred! I truly did make a remarkable catch one scorching day on the UT-Austin campus—one so incredible that no one present believed it. Now, future generations will understand how I pulled off a one-in-a-million feat; here's the miracle in black and white. This was written July 31, 2003.*

# The True Story of the Greatest Catch Ever Made

All right, this might sound like bragging a bit, but I made the greatest catch in the history of football. Human or electric.

You have to take my word for it, of course. This catch was so remarkable, so improbable that not only did my opponents not believe it, but my own teammates disputed that I caught that football.

But I did! Only God and I know it. But I did.

Here's the story:

It was the fall of 1974 when the world was a better place. Well, the Watergate scandal had just come to its slimy end. (On the plus side, we now had a former football player running the country.) The Cowboys missed the playoffs for the first time since 1965. And, climbing the music charts en route to No. 1 was "Kung Fu Fighting" by Carl Douglas.

Hmm, maybe that wasn't the greatest year—good thing I made "The Catch" as we (well, me) called it before the '49ers stole it in '81.

My friend Steve McQueen (okay, right there I'm sure you're doubting this story, but that was his real name) and I played pickup sandlot football games our entire freshman year at UT-Austin. I don't know how we squeezed in any classes.

There were two places to play: The Astroturf practice field or the fake surface at Memorial Stadium. Naturally, the latter was preferred—the Horns played there!—and I'm glad to let you know that The Catch took place at the same location the great Earl Campbell (no relation) rumbled around on.

We were in the middle of a sandlot frenzy—several games were being played at the same time all over the Memorial turf. We had an unspoken code: Games were played on specific sections of the field (usually 20 yards) *across* the field. You did not infringe on neighboring contests.

On this golden afternoon, I was barefoot as usual, having gotten used to the fact that my big right toe— stumped on the fake field back in August—felt a little better without a shoe then with one. So, I played barefoot, somehow tolerating the scorching surface that soaked up the sun.

I played on the skins team. My shoulder-length hair (sans gray) flowed majestically. Except for being just 5-9, 150 pounds with every rib visible, I was pretty much a Greek god.

Okay, we're on the Memorial field. A receiver, my pattern was to run a buttonhook. Who knew this simple route would result in (unheralded) greatness?

I went to the center of our shortened field and curled back to my quarterback. He was under pressure, so I hooked even more. He threw the ball my way. No one disputes these facts.

But what happened next ...

The pass was short, very short. I kept running back toward it, finally leaving my feet then reaching down and forward at the same time. Got that? I'm running, diving forward and downward, headfirst, arms outstretched.

Not touching any part of the Earth with any part of my body, I get to the football when it's about an inch off the ground. I get my fingers under it; the football never scraped the Astroturf. I swear!

So, right now I'm doing a near-handstand except I'm catapulting forward. Very *Matrix*-y. Imagine a bungee jump, head down, arms stretched downward, and snatching something thrown just before it hits the water's surface.

My momentum sent my legs over my head, but I managed to keep the football off the ground. I flipped, almost landing on my back, the ball still securely in my hands.

No one believed the ball did not touch the ground. Not even Steve McQueen. I protested; after all, no one wants to get deprived of the greatest catch ever made. But I was.

I caught it! I did! Just ask God when you get up there. He'll vouch for me. Then I'll say: "Take that Steve McQueen! (*pause*) No, not you—the other one."

195

*I almost didn't run this. I pulled it because it seemed too stupid. But a workmate thought it was a good idea, so I put it back in. Looking at it now, that was the right call. It's kind of cute—even if in 20 years people will wonder what the heck these archaic hieroglyphics were. This was written Aug. 2, 2017.*

# What if Social Media Existed for Historic Events?

Remember the good ol' days when you could get away with something? Nowadays, there's someone filming you or snooping about you on the internet then posting their findings for millions to read—findings that may or may not be true. Imagine if social media had been around for our planet's earlier major events ...

*Huge party at my house to watch that huge asteroid in the sky!*
t-rex   #hardtotypewithsuchdinkyarms

*OMG! Henry the VIII popped the question! I know about his past, but I know I can change him!*
AnnB   #headsup

*Pew-yew! Just watched another endless play by Shakespeare. Something about a chick killing herself for some dude or something! So boring! ZZZZZZZ*
CMarlowe   #hellnevermakeit

*What's up with all that racket outside??!! Somebody's riding by on a horse every 10 minutes shouting that the British are*

*coming! We ARE the British! Shut up already!! Some of us have to work at the tea factory tomorrow!*
Loyalist  #imgonnapunchpaulrevereifiseehimtomorrow

*I just snuck onto the TITANIC! Fake mustache worked! Gonna party every night until I get to the Big Apple!*
Jack  #imgonnaliveforever

*Heard some group called the Beatles (how dumb a name is that!) needs a drummer. PASS!*
SammyMcSnare  #hermanshermitsforever

*Far out! We landed on the moon! We'll be on other planets by 1990! Where do I sign up?!!*
GRoddenberry  #startrekking

*Yo! Had a chance to star in some movie called STAR WARS or something as some guy called Han Solo?! How goofy is that? Looks stupid. No thanks.*
Sly  #workingonaboxingmoviescriptcalledrocky

*Some nerd keeps contacting me to buy stock in something called Apple.*
JQPublic  #homecomputerswillnevercatchon

*Trump for president!? Har! Har! Don't make me laugh!*
HRodham  #nowayicouldeverlose

Mark K. Campbell is the editor of this paper and can't stand social media spelling shortcuts.

*You never know when a column will give someone a chuckle. The week after this ran, a lady wrote to me and said she was waffling about deciding whether to renew her subscription to the paper. Then she read the* Star Trek *reference and said the laugh she got was the difference maker—she reupped. This was written May 24, 2017.*

# The Laying of Hands Versus the Slaying of Toes

Oh, man, this was a rookie deacon mistake.

At my church, we sometimes lay hands on needy folks. This time it was a couple of men—one with chronic pain and the other with a mysterious ailment.

Even before I got to the meeting, I had spent the afternoon working at an estate sale and not only had not been home all day but was wearing the same clothes I had worn earlier to church; I had sweated substantially at the sale and was pretty sure I did not smell my best.

Anyway, our group of 30 or so deacons gathered around the seated men. Because so many deacons are old—at 60, I'm a young buck—I try to assume a hands-on position they might have trouble maintaining.

Like kneeling. So, I did that, placing my hand on the thigh of the man who was experiencing so much pain.

However, I didn't truly kneel; I kinda squatted and immediately regretted my left foot not being flat on the floor but raised on my toes.

Before I could adjust, the praying began. Old men are great at praying and lots joined in, imploring for relief for these two men before us.

My toes began killing me. Shifting around seemed inappropriate, especially since other guys had their hands on me. I tried hard to concentrate on what was being said — the beseeching for these men's sake for some comfort ... and a maybe a little bit for me now.

The prayers continued and my toes were absolutely on fire. I did everything I could to focus on the important chore at hand, but soon I was sweating (again) and could only wonder what my fellow deacons who had their hands on me were thinking: "Man, that guy's really praying — look at him sweat!"

That's when I became aware of the ailing man whose thigh I was laying hands on. While I was struggling with my distal digits, I had unconsciously put an iron-claw grip on his thigh. If I were Mr. Spock, the man would've been unconscious several minutes ago.

The praying continued which was good for the troubled men and bad for this distressed deacon. Finally, it was just too much. I shifted to save my toes. That set off a chain reaction of shifting and shuffling which fortunately did not deter the praying or send deacons falling like dominoes.

At last, the event ended. I staggered up, sweating and toe-numb, praying I did not add to the pain the man was feeling — even as we both limped away.

Mark K. Campbell is the editor of this paper and will stand next time.

*Let's face it: Vegetarians are really proud of being vegetarians—and they'll tell you so. Often. So, an article I read inspired me to note that, if they'd do their part, vegetarians could aid in climate change—by eating meat! I just let this column go where it went; it wasn't the only gas-emission column I'd ever pen, certainly. This was written Nov. 12, 2015.*

# If You Love the Earth, You'll Eat More Hamburgers

Sorry about this, militant vegetarians, but if you really think that meat is murder, you've got a big decision to make.

Because of cows. Forget cars and hair spray—the primary culprit of global warming is gassy bovines. Clearly, we need to start eating many more of them; vegetarians are going to have to step up to save our planet.

If we can get cow expulsions under control, then maybe my asthma inhaler will go back to $5 instead of $30—a change forcing companies to use a new puffer propellant (the old one was apparently terrorizing the ozone) jacked up the price.

The problem with cows is that they emit 200 liters of methane gas every day. Since I live in the United States, I'm not too sure how much that actually is in American, but it sounds like a lot. (In liquid measurement, it's over 52 gallons.)

Anyway, there are over 1.8 *billion* cows going to town—gas- and poop-wise—on the Earth every day, so if my math is correct, that's a lot of methane spewing out of various bovine orifices.

Something has got to be done about these cows. Let's eat 'em!

According to climate change experts (probably), if we all would eat a bunch of cows, we'd quit having hurricanes and terrible droughts. (Maybe I should Google that.)

This is where vegetarians are going to thwart my fellow carnivores' effort to save our blue planet if they don't get with the program.

I can eat a lot of cow meat, but, after a few hundred million pounds, I'm probably going to fall out. Vegetarians are going to have to do their part.

In a 2014 study (Googled!), it was discovered that cows are responsible for 13 million tons of methane annually. By contrast, oil and gas contributed 7 million in that time frame. (Glenn Beck just did a happy backflip.)

Another bonus for vegetarians eating cows is that there'd be more food for vegetarians since the fewer critters (the cows, I mean) will be leaving much more plant life for vegetarians to consume.

It's a win-win for them (the vegetarians, I mean), really. Knock back a few zillion burgers and then it's all-you-can-eat plants forever.

Now, other animals are responsible for gas emissions, too, and I don't mean just firefighters.

Each sheep will fire out 17.6 pounds of gas every year and pigs 3.3 pounds. Pigs are already under the knife of public opinion since bacon is reported to be linked to cancer. At least, that's what experts said last week.

The average human emits 0.26 pounds of gaseous funk annually. (The Bride will attest that I have had days when I reached that mark by noon.) Humans are lightweights.

Some say the key to reducing methane gas emissions is fixing cows' stomachs so they can digest better. Surely, someone at Texas A&M is working on combining hay with Tums or Maalox.

There, I just fixed global warming. You're welcome.

Mark K. Campbell is the editor of this paper and actually prefers Gas-X.

*These catalogues kept arriving at the house, and the different shades of clothes colors seemed ridiculous. I thought of a couple of goofy ones, wrote them down, then figured out some more later on. My boss didn't get what I was going for until his children explained it to him. (I guess that's good?) The Elaine comment refers to the TV episodes where she worked on a catalogue. This was written Dec. 13, 2001.*

# Color My World

Do you know what "Loden" is?

If you do, then you are a woman, an interior decorator, and/or a writer for the L.L. Bean catalogue.

One purchased item from that outdoors outfitters has kept the catalogues a-comin'. They have some pretty cool stuff—rugged pants, jackets, you name it. What they also have is a vivid imagination.

For instance, throughout the catalogue, many kinds of attire are blue. And, wow, do they have some blues! Go ahead: See how many different kinds of blues you can name. Let's see...navy, royal, baby, and maybe denim; that's the best I could do.

Did you get to 18? L.L. Bean did in their holiday book. Here they are: Storm; Navy; True Navy; Mariner; Carbon; Denim; Sky; Royal; Mallard; China; Rangeley (just some guy who got really cold one day?); Steel; Ice; Cobalt; Teal; Medium, Spruce; and French.

As if that wasn't enough, the catalogue is littered with strange names for colors. Somewhere, someone (maybe Elaine from *Seinfeld*) is laughing at what they just read.

There is Olive and Dusty Olive. There's Cabin Red, Vintage Red, and New Red (patterned after the old New Coke?). Like Green? How about Deep Sea Green, Peat Green, Evergreen, Kiwi, Lake, and Stem Green?

In some cases, you can't even tell what the color is being referred to. Sure, you can get the idea when it comes to Winter Wheat, Saddle, and Charcoal. But, they all aren't so easy …

Take a guess at these colors: Thyme; Balsam; Peony; Tarragon; Nightshade; Sage; and the perennial favorite Ocher.

- Thyme—bland green
- Balsam—kinda blue/green
- Peony—bright pink/red
- Tarragon—puke green
- Nightshade—purplish
- Sage—a pale green (man, like blues, they have a lot of greens, too)
- Ocher—sorta tan

You can imagine going to a construction site and hearing, "Hey, Bruno, that Ocher and Balsam shirt really brings out your eyes. Gimme a hug!"

Then there's Natural. In the catalogue, it's a light neutral color. But what if you're black? Or Asian? Then Natural is anything but.

It seems only fair to help out the brilliant minds at L.L. Bean.

Here are some I'd recommend for future catalogues:

- Stumped Toe Purple
- Sinus Infection Green
- Cat Hairball Brown
- Arterial Cut Red
- Home Alone Puppy Yellow

- Chew Your Meat Better Blue
- Allergic to Shellfish Red
- How Hot Was That Chili! Orange

Finally, we arrive at Loden. It's a "non-dusty" Olive Green wool material used in coats. But, personally, I prefer Knocked Out Unconscious White—it's my Natural color.

*This column was another that won multiple awards, including my only accolade from the Houston Press Club. The piece mentions that I had fired off another, much more explicit essay that would never get published and that's true. Even the local underground Big City newspaper where I had published before wouldn't touch it. I tried to not get preachy too often—I usually targeted those holier-than-thou sorts—but I did this time. This was written April 17, 2013.*

# The Word That Will Not Die (Hint: It Starts With 'N')

I'm white. There's some Oklahoma Cherokee in there and some other stuff too, certainly, but mostly I'm Scottish—and super white. And, I'm a multi-generational Texan. Heck, I'm not just white but double white, Southern Baptist deacon white.

I say all this before addressing the giant N-word elephant in the nation's room because this is the perspective of an old white guy who, while just a boy during the Civil Rights movement, still has distinct recollections of it.

A white guy who played football with "black" guys—this was pre-"African-American"—and we went through a mini-civil rights issue of our own on the Meridian, Texas gridiron in the fall of 1973.

A white dude who went to UT-Austin in the mid-70's when there was still plenty peace, love, and happiness between the races and where liberal, groovy professors began instilling the "white guilt" in Baby Boomers that remains prevalent today.

So, here's one old white guy's thinking on the N-word today.

It's not like the word can be avoided. From movies like *Django Unchanged* and *42* to the controversy concerning the country-rap song "Accidental Racist" to tweets from today's teens, the N-word has returned to American conversation big time.

I think the funniest thing I ever wrote is something I can likely never publish. It's a detailed history of a poor white kid who grew up on the Weatherford Traffic Circle in Fort Worth then small-town Texas and how the N-word wove through his life—and how he came to despise it and tried to teach his children to do the same.

And how a generational society shift appears to have thwarted him in that final effort.

Growing up, I heard the N-word all the time from my family and relatives. It was barked when a dark-skinned Dallas Cowboy messed up or when someone dared to get "uppity." It seemed to contrast—sometimes violently—with what I was seeing and hearing elsewhere in my life.

On TV, lots of white folks were marching around the nation with black folks seeking equality.

And on the radio, much of the music I loved through the years was from black artists from Motown or rockers like Jimi Hendrix. Heck, the first 45 rpm single I ever bought was, well, Deep Purple's "Hush," but the second was James Brown's "Papa's Got a Brand New Bag."

It was tough for a boy to hear one thing at home and another from TV and the radio. The N-word was uttered in my Fort Worth elementary schools, too—usually at recess.

I was a reader as a kid and finally learned enough to know that the N-word served no purpose. So, I announced that I would never use it. And I didn't.

A move to a small-town high school challenged that vow, but I made it. Then it was off to UT where I was instilled with WGD (white guilt disease).

I spent my children's young lives training my daughters that that word was unnecessary and divisive and would not be tolerated. I never heard them say it. Until ...

The phone rang, and it was for my teenage daughter. I passed it to her, and her greeting was, "What's up, my N-word?" (But it wasn't "N-word.")

I almost passed out.

When chastised, she said, "Oh, Dad. That's just how we talk today. It's just a word to my generation."

Maybe it *is* just a word. I had to quit following some local white high school athletes on Twitter because they regularly refer to themselves as N-words.

Most rap concerts by African-American artists are attended in great majority by young, white males. And, when the N-word comes up in a lyric during singalongs, there's no flinching as Anglos N-word it up.

That word still shocks me. But then, I'm just a double-white old man, separated from knowing what's going on by two generations now.

Bill Cosby and Oprah—"safe" blacks for us white folks—truly detest the word. Cosby's rants in his old age about how African-Americans have regressed from the hard-earned advances via the brutal struggles of the 60's are popular Facebook fodder for conservative whites.

When filling with gas as a teen, I used to leave the 8-track player cranked to Hendrix's "Crosstown Traffic." Now, the stuff I hear from nearby cars fueling at RaceTrac contain horribly misogynistic and straight-up vile lyrics, often filled with the N-word.

So, what's a double-white guy to do? I tried to teach my kids to not say the N-word. I tried; I guess I'll die with WGD.

Maybe I'll write a rap song using Ephesians 4:29—*Let no unwholesome talk come out of your mouths, but only what is helpful for building others up according to their needs, that it may benefit those who listen.*

Word to your mother. And everybody else.

Mark K. Campbell is the editor of this paper and knows most of "Bust a Move."

*This is, without question, one of my favorite columns of all-time. After I heard a preacher discuss this seldom-heard incident in the Bible, I couldn't get to my computer fast enough. And, yes, it's pun filled, as you'd expect. This was written Aug. 29, 2018.*

# The Bible Story You Likely Haven't Heard Before

I have attended church for decades, and I've heard and read a zillion stories from the Good Book.

Tales of hope and redemption and war and horror and miracles and tragedy and love and just about every other topic you can imagine presented in allegory, poetry, imagery, onomatopoeia, parables, symbolism, and straightforward storytelling.

With such a wide array of tales told in a plethora of literary devices, it's no wonder that the Bible is the best-selling book of all time.

Yes, I figured I'd consumed at least something about every event in the Bible among the 31,000-plus verses and 700,000 words—until I heard about … the golden hemorrhoids.

It's quite a story with the underlying theme being how things will not go well for you if you disrespect what God says.

The Old Testament adventure of the golden hemorrhoids can be found in 1 Samuel, Chapters 4-7.

(Before we get started and you begin writing your angry Letters to the Editor, some Biblical scholars believe it wasn't actually hemorrhoids at the seat of this story; some versions say "tumors" and others think it might be the "bubonic plague" that torment so many—however, the King James version clearly says "smitten with emerods" so ...)

Here's what happened:

The Philistines and Israelites went to war, and the latter took it in the shorts big time the first go-round. Hebrew generals who stayed behind figured the best way to beat the Philistines was to pull out their ace in the hole—the Ark of the Covenant.

That fired up the remaining Israelite troops and freaked out the Philistines who "fought like men," battling for their very lives against the undefeated Ark of the Covenant.

Not only did the Philistines win again—killing 30,000 Israelites—but the victors stole the Ark!

The Philistines toted their prize back to Ashrod and stashed it next to their chosen god, Dagon.

Checking on it the next day, it was discovered that Dagon, who was half man, half fish, had fallen over.

They stood Dagon back up. The next day, not only had it been toppled again before the Ark, but the god's head and arms were both snapped off.

Oh, it was about to get a whole lot worse.

Soon, 30,000 Philistines in Ashrod were smitten with emerods. That, as you can imagine, caused a run on Preparation B (they hadn't gotten to H yet), and soon there was a great gnashing of teeth and clothes renting.

It didn't take long for Ashrodians to say, "Get that Ark out of here!" They shipped it out to the town of Gath where another 30,000 got emerods.

Then, the Ark got punted to Ekron who surely said, "Yeah, I don't think so!" (Even before the days of social media, an event like this traveled fast.)

And the emerod event happened in Ekron, too, prompting smart Philistine leaders to decide to send the Ark back to the Israelites. (Being politicians, it took six months for them to get off their booties and do something.)

Not only did they decide to return the Ark, but they wanted to give a "trespass offering" to make sure the Hebrews accepted it.

The decision was made to create five golden emerods as well as five golden mice "according to the number of lords of the Philistines." (Since mice carry fleas which carry bubonic plague, here's where some anti-hemorrhoid scholars go that route.)

The Ark was put on a cart and eventually made its way back home.

Along the way, a bunch of people who dared to peek inside the Ark died—even though God had always said to *never do that!*

And the Ark got parked for 20 years at a guy's house. Then all of Israel's fake gods had to be gotten rid of. *Then* the Ark was returned to its proper place.

Eventually, Israel defeated the Philistines who were, perhaps, still hobbled by their terrible hemorrhoidal woes— or maybe really worried that it could happen again.

Either way, I can only imagine that Grandpa Ramathaimzophim had quite a story to tell at the family reunion.

Mark K. Campbell is the editor of this paper and never thought he would write the words "anti-hemorrhoid scholars."

Made in the USA
Columbia, SC
16 November 2024

45936152R00124